DEVELOPMENT OF THE SYNTAX-DISCOURSE INTERFACE

STUDIES IN THEORETICAL PSYCHOLINGUISTICS

VOLUME 23

Managing Editors

Lyn Frazier, *Dept. of Linguistics, University of Massachusetts at Amherst*

Thomas Roeper, *Dept. of Linguistics, University of Massachusetts at Amherst*

Kenneth Wexler, *Dept. of Brain and Cognitive Science, MIT, Cambridge, Mass.*

Editorial Board

Robert Berwick, *Artifical Intelligence Laboratory, MIT, Cambridge, Mass.*

Manfred Bierwisch, *Zentralinstitut für Sprachwissenschaft, Akademie der Wissenschaften, Berlin*

Merrill Garrett, *University of Arizona, Tucson*

Lila Gleitman, *School of Education, University of Pennsylvania*

Mary-Louise Kean, *University of California, Irvine*

Howard Lasnik, *University of Connecticut at Storrs*

John Marshall, *Neuropsychology Unit, Radcliffe Infirmary, Oxford*

Daniel Osherson, *M.I.T., Cambridge, Mass.*

Yukio Otsu, *Keio University, Tokyo*

Edwin Williams, *Princeton University*

The titles published in this series are listed at the end of this volume.

DEVELOPMENT OF THE SYNTAX-DISCOURSE INTERFACE

by

SERGEY AVRUTIN
*Yale University,
New Haven, CT, U.S.A.*

KLUWER ACADEMIC PUBLISHERS
DORDRECHT / BOSTON / LONDON

Library of Congress Cataloging-in-Publication Data

ISBN 0-7923-5936-4

Published by Kluwer Academic Publishers,
P.O. Box 17, 3300 AA Dordrecht, The Netherlands.

Sold and distributed in North, Central and South America
by Kluwer Academic Publishers,
101 Philip Drive, Norwell, MA 02061, U.S.A.

In all other countries, sold and distributed
by Kluwer Academic Publishers,
P.O. Box 322, 3300 AH Dordrecht, The Netherlands.

Printed on acid-free paper

All Rights Reserved
© 1999 Kluwer Academic Publishers
No part of the material protected by this copyright notice may be reproduced or
utilized in any form or by any means, electronic or mechanical,
including photocopying, recording or by any information storage and
retrieval system, without written permission from the copyright owner.

Printed in the Netherlands.

To Dasha and Matvei

TABLE OF CONTENTS

Acknowledgements xi

Introduction 1

Chapter I
Establishing Reference 8
1. Introduction 8
2. Pronominals in Adult and Child Speech 10
   2.1. Pronominals in Natural Languages 10
   2.2. Previous Acquisition Results 16

Chapter II
Syntax, Discourse and Interpretation of Pronominals 23
1. General Model 23
2. Syntactic Constraints and Interpretation of Indices 25
3. File Change Semantics 30
4. Interpretation of Indices in Syntax and Discourse 32
5. Various Uses of Definite NPs 38
6. Incorporation and Accommodation 42
7. Constraints on Bridging 50

Chapter III
Anomalous Indexation 54
1. Principle A and Principle B Constructions 54
2. Good Performance with Pronouns 60

TABLE OF CONTENTS

3. Weak Pronouns — 64
4. Principle C Constructions — 66

Chapter IV
Experimental Evidence for the Proposed Model — 69

1. Experimental Evidence for the Existence of two Different Mechanisms: Incorporation and Accommodation — 69
2. Deictic Use of Definite NPs in Children's Discourse — 72
   2.1 Pronominalization in Children's Discourse — 72
   2.2 Children's Use of R-expressions — 74
3. Limitations of Inferential Capacity — 78

Chapter V
Possessive Pronouns and Reflexives in Russian — 83

1. Overview of Russian Possessives — 83
2. Experimental Results — 85

Chapter VI
Plural Pronouns — 93

1. Distributivity and Binding in Child Grammar — 93
2. Plural Pronouns — 95
3. Experiment — 97
4. Results — 100
5. Conclusions — 101

TABLE OF CONTENTS ix

Chapter VII
Children's Interpretation of the Discourse-dependent Reflexives 103
1. The Standard Binding Theory, Reflexivity and Logophors 105
2. Locative PPs and "Picture NPs" 111
3. General Method 116
   3.1 Experiment 1: Reflexives in Locative PPs 117
   3.2 Experiment Two: Reflexives in "Picture NPs" 125
4. Conclusions 129

Chapter VIII
Discourse-Based Analyses of Root Infinitives 131
1. The Data 132
2. Hyams' Underspecification Theory of Root Infinitives 135
3. Root Infinitives in Adult Russian 138
   3.1. The Role of Indices in the Representation of NPs, Tenses and Events 140
   3.2. Discourse Representation of Russian Root Infinitives 144
   3.3. Further Constraints on Russian RIs 149
4. The Headline Register 152
5. Mad Magazine Register 158

6.	Achievement Predicates, Perfective Constructions, and Pronouns in Tenseless Clauses	159
	6.1 Achievement Predicates	160
	6.2 Perfective Constructions	161
	6.3 Pronouns in Tenseless Clauses	162
7.	The Optional Infinitive Stage	165
	7.1 Presuppositional Introduction of an Event File Card	165
	7.2 Null Subject Languages	169
8.	Root Infinitives in the speech of Broca's aphasics	172

Chapter IX
Summary and Concluding Remarks 176
1. The Limitation of Processing Resources as an Explanation of Linguistic Performance 176
2. Child Language and Aphasia 179

Notes 184

References 193

Index 207

ACKNOWLEDGEMENTS

This book is a thorough revision and extension of my Ph.D. dissertation from the Massachusetts Institute of Technology. First and foremost, therefore, I would like to thank my adviser Kenneth Wexler for his help, advice and encouragement. I am also grateful to David Pesetsky, a member of my dissertation committee, for his guidance and important suggestions throughout my work. Thanks are also due to Steven Pinker and Suzanne Carey for their comments on earlier versions of my dissertation.

I would like to thank my teachers at Brandeis University and MIT: Noam Chomsky, Jane Grimshaw, Kenneth Hale, Irene Heim, James Higginbotham, Ray Jackendoff, Alec Marantz, Molley Potter, Alan Prince, Tanya Reinhart, Edgar Zurif.

Several projects reported in this book were conducted in collaboration with Stella Ceytlin, Stephen Crain, Jennifer Cunningham, Jennifer Green, Stuart Lubarsky, Rozalind Thornton. Their friendship and help are also much appreciated. I am grateful to Josef Aoun, Maria Babyonyshev, Roelien Bastianse, Peter Coopmans, Martin Everaert, Danny Fox, Herman Kolk, Howard Lasnik, Orin Percus, Colin Phillips, Eric Reuland, and Maaike Verrips for their comments on various parts of this book, and would like to thank my former colleagues at University of Pennsylvania and my colleagues at Yale University: Stephen Anderson, Lila Gleitman, Louis Goldstein, Laurence Horn, Stanley Insler, Dianne Jonas, Abigail Kaun, Ellen Prince. Very special thanks are due to Maarten Janssen for his assistance in my continuous struggle with the word processor. The recommendations of anonymous reviewers have greatly aided me in the preparation of this book.

At various stages, I was supported in part by a National Institute of Health research grant P50 DC 00081 and a grant from the International Research and Exchanges Board with funds provided by the National Endowment for the Humanities, the US Department of State, and the

ACKNOWLEDGEMENTS

US Information Agency. None of these organisations is responsible for the views expressed.

And, of course, to Dasha and Matvei -- many thanks for making my life more interesting!

INTRODUCTION

In this book, I address several issues of child linguistic development from the perspective of the syntax - discourse interface. Traditionally, language acquisition research has focused on the development of one of the linguistic modules, e.g. acquisition of syntax, morphology or phonology. While this approach can be viewed as fruitful in some cases, there is a number of linguistic phenomena whose explanation depends on the interaction of different modules and, therefore, different domains of linguistic knowledge. A typical example is pronominal anaphora: It can be shown that to correctly use pronominal elements, normal adult speakers must possess both syntactic and pragmatic knowledge, and that these kinds of knowledge must interact with each other.

With regard to the language acquisition process, such phenomena suggest a somewhat different approach to the language acquisition research. Indeed, if some experimental studies show that children make errors in the construction under investigation, it will be necessary to consider these results from the point of view of the interaction of the different domains of linguistic knowledge involved in their interpretation. In other words, if this particular construction requires the integration of, for example, syntactic and discourse-based knowledge, children's errors may, in principle, be due to their lack of the former, the latter, or both kinds of knowledge, and cannot be taken as direct evidence for the "underdeveloped" status of just one of them.

Another question that will be directly relevant for the studies discussed in this book is whether the errors demonstrated by children (in experimental settings or in natural speech) are due to the *lack of knowledge* of certain linguistic principles, or to their *inability to implement* this knowledge. Without answering this question, the picture of a normal language development cannot be complete and accurate. Furthermore, if it can be argued that children do posses all relevant knowledge but cannot always use it, it is desirable to have an explanation for this psycholinguistic deficit. The most intuitively plausible explanation seems to be that children do not have enough processing recourses (in the sense that should be made precise) to correctly analyse certain constructions, which results in their apparently abnormal responses or ungrammatical utterances. The learnability problem (in the sense that children need to figure out the correct grammar from the input) does not arise in this case: Children will demonstrate an adult-like pattern of responses when their processing capacity matures. Of course, to obtain a full picture of linguistic development, it will be necessary, at some point, to say something more specific about development of processing capacity. At this point, however, I will limit myself to an intuitive understanding that the human brain matures and, therefore, its processing capacity grows.

In this regard, it is sometimes interesting and useful to compare certain errors observed in experiments with children with those demonstrated by brain-damaged patients, specifically agrammatic Broca's aphasics. In this book, I present results of several studies in which these patients demonstrated results very similar to those obtained in acquisition experiments. Moreover, in those constructions where children demonstrate an adult-like performance, Broca's aphasics also show a significantly better pattern of responses. I will argue that these similarities between children and aphasics on the one hand, and their differences from normal adult speakers, on the other, can be explained assuming that these populations lack necessary processing recourses while possessing all relevant linguistic knowledge. In particular, I will suggest that certain constructions requiring the integration of syntactic and discourse - based knowledge require more resources than constructions requiring syntactic knowledge only. As a result, both children and aphasics demonstrate a significantly better performance on the "syntax - only" type of constructions.

In this book, therefore, I will discuss several experiments carried out with children and, in some cases, with agrammatic Broca's aphasics. These results will be analysed from the perspective of the syntax - discourse interface. Consistent with the recent developments in the linguistic theory (e.g. Chomsky's Minimalist Program), the understanding of interface conditions (in this case the interface between syntax and discourse) is important for coherent analyses of a variety of psycholinguistic studies.

Before proceeding any further, it is important to emphasise what this book is and is not about. As most of the data discussed in this book are *abnormal* linguistic data (that is, errors made by children and/or brain-damaged people), two questions arise: (i) What part of the linguistic (or non-linguistic) system does the deficit belong to? and (ii) Given a specific deficit, how does it explain the experimental data? For example, suppose a child (or an aphasic patient) exhibits problems with verbal affixes. Is this a problem related to morphology or syntax? What is the morphological, or syntactic, deficit that explains the observed problem?

In the case of the syntax-discourse interface development, the first step, too, is to identify whether the problem belongs to the syntax, to the discourse, or to the interface between the two. In my view, the theoretical apparatus for the analyses of the syntactic part is much more sophisticated than the theoretical machinery for discourse analyses. It is inevitable then that there will be a certain vagueness with respect to the analyses of what exactly happens at the discourse level. In this book, therefore, I will focus primarily on the first question: I will concentrate, throughout the book, on identifying the area responsible for the errors observed in children and aphasics. Specifically, I will argue that, at least in the case discussed here, their syntactic knowledge is intact but the problems belong to the level of discourse, or to the interface between syntax and discourse. The second question, that is how the putative deficit explains the observed errors, will be addressed in some depth only in the case of pronominal interpretation (Chapters III, IV, V and VI). Regarding analyses of logophors (Chapter VII) and Root Infinitives (Chapter VIII), my main goal will be to argue for the non-syntactic nature of the observed deficit, that is to simply outline the domain where, as I will claim, the deficit is located. In the absence of a well-developed theoretical apparatus for the analyses of logophoricity, or temporal discourse anaphora, the question of what exactly happens in discourse in the case of children and aphasics can be answered only vaguely. Thus, the main goal of Chapters 7 and 8 will be to identify the location of the observed deficit.

The book is organised as follows. In Chapter I, I formulate the question addressed in the following chapters, namely what kind of knowledge is required for the correct interpretation of pronominal elements. It will be shown that, unlike R-expressions, the interpretation of pronominals depends on certain syntactic (structural) properties of the sentence. At the same time, referring pronouns (unlike those interpreted as bound variables and unlike reflexives) also rely in their interpretation on the discourse conditions. Thus, pronominal elements differ with respect to whether their interpretation requires only syntactic knowledge, or the integration of syntax and discourse. In this Chapter, I also present a brief summary of previous experimental results with children regarding their interpretation of pronominals.

In Chapter II, I present elements of the File Change Semantics (Heim 1982) as a model of the discourse representation of NPs. An indefinite NP in this theory is represented in the discourse with a new file card, while a definite NP does not introduce a new file card (normally) but is incorporated into an existing one. Developing Heim's theory somewhat further, I show that the syntax - discourse interface conditions can be expressed in terms of the instantiation of the variable index on an NP with a number of a file card in the discourse. I show how this model accommodates the well-known distinction between *sense* and *reference*, for example the fact that one referent can have two different senses (or *guises*). A file card, thus, should be taken to represent a guise rather than a referent of a certain NP. I also discuss the cases of *Accommodation* as another mechanism of introducing a definite NP into discourse. This mechanism is closely related to the notion of *bridging* also discussed in this Chapter. Finally, I show how this model can be extended to incorporate the deictic use of definite NPs and discuss the constraints on bridging as a discourse-based operation.

In Chapter III, I return to the analyses of the errors demonstrated by children in the so-called Principle B studies. I show, in agreement with Chien and Wexler 1992, that children do have all relevant knowledge, specifically they do know Principle B of the Binding Theory, but their problem is related to the syntax - discourse interface. I analyse their errors from the point of view of the theory outlined in Chapter II, and show how this approach predicts a different pattern of responses to referring pronouns on the one hand, and reflexives and pronouns as bound variables, on the other. I also discuss children's good performance on sentences with weak pronouns and Principle C constructions.

In Chapter IV, I present evidence from various psycholinguistic studies that supports the proposed model of the syntax - discourse interface. This evidence comes from real - time studies with normal adults, studies of the use of deictic pronouns in children, children's construction and comprehension of discourse, and their use of definite R-expressions. I also briefly discuss children's (and aphasics') ability to interpret contrastive stress. I argue that the results of these studies show that the discourse - based operations require additional processing resources, which children and aphasics may lack. The processing approach, thus, provides a coherent explanation for a variety of apparently unrelated studies across different constructions with different populations.

In Chapter V, I turn to the theoretical and experimental investigations of Russian possessive pronouns and their interpretation by Russian - speaking children. First, I briefly present a theory developed in Avrutin (1994) that explains the distribution of possessive pronouns and reflexives in Russian. The approach adopted in this work is the "movement" analyses: Russian pronominals (in some cases) are argued to undergo LF movement to a functional projection, which may result in a violation of Principle B. In this chapter, I also present results of an experimental study with Russian speaking children that addresses their knowledge of the relevant constraints on the interpretation of Russian pronominals. The results, consistent with previous findings, show once again the distinction between good performance in the "syntax - only" conditions, vs. chance performance in "syntax and discourse" conditions. The obtained results are discussed in the framework of the theory proposed in previous chapters.

In Chapter VI, I discuss a theory of the collective and distributive interpretation of plural pronouns as developed by Heim, Lasnik and May (1991). In this theory, pronouns interpreted collectively are referring elements, while pronouns interpreted distributively are variables bound by a distributive operator D. I present results of an acquisition experiment with English speaking children who were shown to be sensitive to this distinction precisely in the way proposed in this book: they demonstrated a significantly better performance on sentences with pronouns interpreted as bound variables than with referring (collective) pronouns.

In Chapter VII, I discuss the cases of non-syntactic, logophoric reflexives, whose interpretation depends not on syntactic Principle A, but on certain discourse - based rules. In particular, I analyse reflexives in Locative PPs and reflexives in "Picture NPs", some of which have been argued to be logophoric (e.g. Reinhart and Reuland 1993). The experimental study reported in this Chapter shows that the distinction between syntactic and discourse - based interpretations established for pronouns in previous chapters holds also for reflexives. English - speaking children demonstrate a significantly better performance with "syntactic" than with logophoric reflexives.

In Chapter VIII, I somewhat extend the proposed analyses to the domain of temporal anaphora. The phenomenon under investigation is the so-called Optional Infinitive stage in child's development (Wexler 1994) where children acquiring (non-pro-drop) languages are shown to incorrectly allow non-finite verbs in the main clauses. I address this issue from two directions. First, I demonstrate that under certain discourse constrained circumstances, these constructions are also allowed in adult speech. In this regard, I provide a theory of the Russian infinitival constructions (labelled the "Princess sentences"), English headlines, and the so-called English Mad Magazine register. All these registers allow untensed verbs in the main clauses. I further discuss the acquisition data in the framework of the theory of infinitives in adult speech and propose an account based on the idea of insufficient processing recourses.

Finally, Chapter IX contains summary and concluding remarks, as well as theoretical considerations of the observed similarities between child and aphasic speech discussed in various places throughout the book

CHAPTER I

ESTABLISHING REFERENCE

1. Introduction

All natural languages contain certain elements whose interpretation depends on their linguistic (and, sometimes, non-linguistic) environment. These elements are pronominals: pronouns and reflexives. The information associated with the lexical entry for, say, pronoun *she* or reflexive *himself*, is limited and is never sufficient to provide a unique interpretation for these elements. The environment where these elements appear functions as a source of information for establishing reference.

The interpretation of pronominals depends both on syntactic, and contextual factors. To correctly interpret the pronoun *she*, which (potentially) can be used to talk about an infinite number of singular female individuals, speakers have to integrate their knowledge of syntactic and discourse-related principles. An important difference between these two kinds of knowledge is that the knowledge of syntactic principles is *speaker-internal*: it represents their internalised knowledge of language. The knowledge of discourse-related principles, by contrast, is *conversation-internal*: it relies (in its implementation) on taking into account other speakers' representation of a given conversation. Given that speakers fluently and effortlessly use pronominals in their conversations, one may conclude that coordination of these two types of knowledge is a natural capacity of normal adult speakers.

In this chapter, I develop a model of the syntax-discourse interface that shows how speakers' syntactic knowledge is coordinated with their knowledge of discourse principles. As the basis for this model, I take two existing theories. From the syntactic side, the Binding Theory (Chomsky 1986), and from the discourse side, File Change Semantics (Heim 1982). These two levels constitute separate, independent levels of representation, each of which is characterised by its own principles. The model I propose aims to explain how these principles interact with each other. More specifically, it relies on indexation of noun phrases and interpretation of this indexation as a mechanism for integrating syntactic and contextual information. I show how syntactic indices are interpreted at the level of discourse to establish reference for noun phrases, in particular pronominals.

Second, I further develop the existing model of discourse to incorporate the deictic use of definite NPs. The idea behind this enterprise is to make a non-linguistic source of reference (deixis) compatible with linguistic sources (e.g. NPs previously mentioned in the discourse). This will be shown to have important consequences for analyses of children's and aphasics' errors in pronominal interpretation.

Third, I show how the proposed model explains results of experiments with children and Broca's aphasics. In many studies, these two populations have been shown to assign a wrong reference to pronouns in certain constructions. Although, on the face of it, they behave as if they lack the knowledge of some linguistic principles, I argue that this is not the case. As mentioned above, establishing reference for a pronoun requires the use of both speaker-internal and conversation-internal knowledge. Further developing the idea proposed in Chien and Wexler (1990), and Avrutin 1994, I argue that children and Broca's aphasics have difficulties implementing the second type of knowledge because it requires making certain inferences about other speakers' representations of the discourse. I show how limitation on processing resources that these two populations exhibit results in a wrong interpretation of indices, in particular in an incorrect use of deixis. Thus, the account I offer claims that children's and aphasics' knowledge of relevant principles is no different from that of normal adults, although their processing capacity is more limited.

I also present results of theoretical and experimental projects. I present results of acquisition experiments with Russian-speaking children. Their responses show that children between the ages of 4 and 6 possess subtle linguistic knowledge necessary for correct interpretation of possessive pronominals. Similarly to previous experiments, however, in those conditions where children had to make inferences about other speakers' representation of discourse, their performance was once again poor.

Overall, the theory and experiments presented in this book argue for a modular account of linguistic development and breakdown. I argue that the relevant linguistic knowledge is available to young children and intact in Broca's aphasics, while their capacity to implement (at least part of) this knowledge is limited. With respect to the development, no learnability question arises on this account. Children will perform like normal adults when their capacity to implement linguistic knowledge has matured. Before that, their responses to experimental conditions may be misinterpreted as a manifestation of lack of knowledge.

2. Pronominals in Adult and Child Speech

2.1. Pronominals in Natural Languages

All languages give their speakers an opportunity to avoid unnecessary repetition of names and other referring expressions by making use of the pronominal system. This system represents a very special interest for linguists and psycholinguists because these elements do not have their own interpretation, and their interpretation depends on the linguistic environment. Speakers, clearly, use and understand pronominals fluently, and, in most cases, interpret them correctly. Thus, from the computational point of view, speakers are able to solve what appears to be a complicated task: to find an appropriate interpretation for an element that on each occasion has a different interpretation depending upon where it appears in the input. Remarkably, as will be discussed in following chapters, such mastery is evident even in young children.

Pronominals have attracted linguists' attention because their interpretation depends on the syntactic environment and reflects, to a certain extent, the structure of a sentence. A simple example illustrates the point. The interpretation of NP *an apple* is the same in (1a) as in (1b); that is, it does not depend on the structure of the sentence. By contrast, the interpretation of the pronoun *her* in (2a) is different from the interpretation of the same pronoun in (2b).

(1) a. Mary thinks that Jane ate an apple.
    b. Mary thinks that Jane's mother ate an apple.
(2) a. Mary thinks that Jane likes her.
    b. Mary thinks that Jane's mother likes her.

In (2a), speakers interpret the pronoun as referring to Mary, and in (2b), it can be either Mary or Jane. Intuitively, the difference between NP *an apple* and NP *her* is that the former carries some independent information used for its interpretation, while the latter carries no such information. All relevant information is encoded in the form of features +singular, +feminine, which may be used to talk about an infinite number of objects. The linguistic environment supplies some additional information, thus making it clear which object is being discussed.

As we can see from (2), however, this information is supplied in a restricted way. That is, the structure of a sentence where a pronoun appears plays a certain role in how it can be interpreted. The same is obviously true about another type of pronominals, i.e. reflexives:

(3) a. Mary thinks that Jane likes herself.
    b. Mary thinks that Jane's mother likes herself.

Once again, the interpretation of the reflexive depends on the structure of the sentence. To be more precise, two linguistic factors play a role in restricting the range of possible interpretations: c-command and locality. In (2a), *Jane* locally c-commands *her*. Thus, it cannot be used as a source of information necessary for interpreting the pronoun due to the syntactic Principle B (see below). A non-local name (*Mary*), on the other hand, can supply the relevant information, as well as a non-c-commanding name (*Jane* in (2b)). The same factors are relevant for reflexives, but in the opposite way: only locally c-commanding NPs can be used to interpret a reflexive. These two factors -- c-command and locality -- have been incorporated in the so-called Binding Principles (Chomsky 1981) Somewhat simplifying the original formulation and focusing only on pronouns and reflexives, these principles can be stated as in (4).

(4) Principle A: Reflexives must be locally bound.
Principle B: Pronouns must be locally free.

An element is said to be bound if it is coindexed with another element that c-commands it. The question of what coindexation represents will be extensively discussed in Chapter II.

Principles A and B are syntactic principles that regulate which NPs *in a given sentence* can potentially be a source of pronominal interpretation. It is clear, however, that pronouns (and reflexives under certain circumstances) can be interpreted even in the absence of any intra-sentential antecedent:

(5) a. I like her. She is smart.
b. I want to talk to HIM, not to HIM (while pointing to someone).
c. John was walking down the street when he met Bill. They talked for a while, and then he suggested they have a drink.

The pronoun *her* in (5a) is interpretable if all participants in a given conversation know that there is some female individual presupposed as a topic of their conversation. It is also interpretable in (5b) if the listener sees who the speaker is pointing to. In (5c), speakers tend to interpret the pronoun as referring to John, although it does not appear in the same sentence, and there is another masculine NP around.[1] The point of these examples is to show that more than syntax alone is involved in interpreting pronominals. It involves both syntactic and discourse information. In this sense, pronominals occupy a very special place in natural languages because their interpretation requires (with the exception of bound variables discussed below) that speakers carry out both syntactic, and discourse-related computations. Moreover, syntactic knowledge is "speaker-internal": it is a reflection of speakers' knowledge of language. The knowledge of discourse rules, by contrast, requires making certain inferences about other participants in the conversation. In (5a), for example, the speaker must make sure that the female individual under discussion is the same for all other speakers. No such inferences are required to know that, in (2a), *her* can (potentially) be Mary, but it can never be Jane. Let us briefly discuss the syntactic conditions on the choice of an antecedent. I defer the discussion of discourse-related factors until Chapter II.

The restrictions on what can be a possible antecedent for a pronoun apparently exist in all languages. Languages may differ, however, with respect to the locality requirement, that is "how far away" from the pronominal its antecedent is allowed to be. For example, in Russian, a reflexive can be bound outside its clause but only if this clause is infinitival. In Icelandic, a reflexive can also be bound outside a subjunctive clause. None of these is allowed in English:

(6) a. Ivan ugovoril Petra sfotografirovat' sebja.
Ivan convinced Peter to photograph himself (Ivan or Peter)
b. Jon vildi ad Petur rakadi sig.
John wants that[SUBJ] Peter shaved self (John or Peter).

Both NPs can be interpreted as an antecedent for the reflexive in (6a,b). Russian possessive pronouns, on the other hand, have less freedom than English possessives:

(7) Ivan pokazal Petru ego komnatu.
Ivan showed (to) Peter his room

In English, the possessive pronoun *his* can be interpreted as either Ivan or Peter, while in Russian *ego* 'his' can only be Peter. Other languages impose yet other locality restrictions on what can be a possible antecedent.

This cross-linguistic variation presents an interesting learnability problem. A child does not know at birth what language it is going to acquire, more specifically, what are the locality restrictions imposed on the choice of an antecedent. The child, presumably, can figure out what is a pronoun, and what is a reflexive, but this knowledge alone is not sufficient to demonstrate an adult-like behavior. As mentioned above, to be interpretable, pronominals need to receive some additional information from their environment, and the child has to figure out where this information can be received from, for example, whether it can be an NP in the same clause.

There have been several proposals in the literature regarding how the child learns what a local domain is in his/her language. Wexler and Manzini (1987), for example, suggest that the locality requirement can be parameterised in such a way that grammatical sentences of one language will form a subset of grammatical sentences of another one. Their theory is based on the Subset Principle (Berwick 1985) whereby children will move from the smaller language to a bigger one when they hear certain constructions in their target language. All children begin with the parameter setting that gives them the most restrictive type of grammar. For example, both English and Russian children begin with a hypothesis that the local domain for a reflexive is the clause. Thus, (6a) in Russian is initially outside the child's grammar on the reading where the reflexive is bound by the matrix subject. When Russian-speaking children hear sentences like (6a), they reset their parameter to such a value that allows binding of reflexives outside an infinitival clause. English-speaking children, on the other hand, never receive this input (because adults never produce such sentences in English), and, therefore, their initial setting of the relevant parameter is, actually, the final one. Thus, this theory provides a model of acquisition of the locality constraint from positive data only. Although this theory has been shown to make wrong predictions with respect to some languages (e.g. Sigurjonsdottir and Hyams 1992 for Icelandic, Baylin 1992 for Russian), it provides an interesting model of acquisition of linguistic knowledge. It is possible that the parameters involved in the formulation of such a theory should be based not on the structural properties of a sentence, but on morphological (X-bar) properties of pronominal elements (whether it is a head or a maximal projection, whether it is a monomorphemic, or a polimorphemic element), but I will not discuss this issue here. Analyses along these lines can be found in Pica 1987, Hestvik 1992, Baylin 1992, Cardinaletti and Starke 1993, among others. In any case, the child has to figure out (from positive data only) the correct setting of certain parameters in order to become a competent speaker of his or her language.

It is interesting that theories that concern themselves with acquisition of constraints on pronominal interpretation provide, in most cases, purely syntactic models. The child, for example, may have to figure out the relevant structural characteristics of the binding domain, or the relevant morphosyntactic property of the element itself. At the same time, as discussed at the beginning of this section, the interpretation of a pronominal element (a pronoun, in particular) depends both on syntactic, and discourse-related factors. It is clear, therefore, that a comprehensive learning model must include both components. It has to specify what syntactic constraints the child has to know, as well as what the child has to know about the discourse that a given sentence is part of. Recently, researchers have begun to attempt to look at the development of pronominal interpretation from both syntactic, and pragmatic (discourse-related) points of view (for example, Foster-Cohen 1994, whose analyses are based on Sperber and Wilson's (1986) Theory of Relevance. In the following section, I briefly discuss previous acquisition results and theories proposed to account for these results. I suggest that a more detailed theory is needed to account for cross-linguistic acquisition data in a coherent way. Such a theory will be presented in Chapters II and III.

2.2. Previous Acquisition Results

Acquisition of a pronominal system represents a very active direction of research in the field of developmental linguistics. During the last decade, quite a few studies have attempted to investigate children's mastery of pronominals, both in English, and in other languages. A very detailed and careful discussion of previous data (as well as corresponding references) is presented in Koster (1993). I will not repeat here results of all the experiments, but rather summarise the cross-linguistic data, and present a pattern that emerges from analyses of these data.

Jakubowitz (1984) first noticed that children's performance is significantly better on sentences with reflexives than on sentences with pronouns. Thus, in a situation where Father Bear washes himself, children almost always correctly accept (8). If Father Bear does not wash himself, but washes somebody else, they correctly reject (8).

(8) Father Bear washed himself.

(Good performance: almost 100% acceptance)

At the same time, children sometimes incorrectly allow (9) as a true description of situation where Father Bear washes himself:

(9) Father Bear washed him.

(Poor performance: about 50% acceptance)

Jakubowitz suggested that children at this age (4-6 years old) incorrectly interpret pronouns as reflexive elements. In English, it could be so because pronouns and reflexives are morphologically similar. This explanation, however, does not hold. First, Avrutin and Wexler (1992) show that Russian speaking children show exactly the same pattern, although Russian pronouns and reflexives are not morphologically similar (for example, Russian *him* is *ego*, and Russian *himself* is *sebja*). Second, if children confused pronouns and reflexives, we might expect them to always accept (9), to be more precise, to accept (9) as often as they accept (8). This, however, does not happen: children demonstrate an almost perfect performance on reflexive conditions, and around chance performance on pronoun conditions. In other words, children are sensitive to the difference between pronouns and reflexives. Moreover, as Grimshaw and Rosen (1990) showed, children demonstrate a very good performance in the "non-coreference" case, that is when Father Bear washes someone else. In this case, children correctly accept (9) almost 100% of the time. This result, of course, is not consistent with the proposal that children may confuse pronouns and reflexives: should it be the case, the responses to the non-coreference case should also be around chance.

Wexler and Chien (1985) questioned Jakubowitz's claim. They argued that children possess all relevant syntactic knowledge (e.g. Principles A and B) and know the difference between pronouns and reflexives. An important insight first offered in this article was that children are different from adults in their treatment of indexation. Wexler and Chien suggest that children's representation of (9) is different from adults' in that *Father Bear* and *him* are allowed to have different indices but be coreferential. I return to this proposal, which was the basis for the "Principle P account", later in this chapter. In this article, Wexler and Chien suggest that children's performance on sentences with quantified antecedents should be good because of the necessary coindexation. This experiment was carried out and is reported in Chien and Wexler (1991). Indeed, children's performance improves significantly when the antecedent for a pronoun is a quantified NP, as in (10).

(10) Every bear washed him.

In contrast to (9), children correctly reject this sentence as a description of a situation where every bear washed himself. If children had difficulties with distinguishing pronouns and reflexives, we should not expect any difference in their responses to (9) and (10). Thus, as Chien and Wexler point out, children are sensitive to the nature of the antecedent, which (as will be discussed below) determines the character of the pronoun (whether it is a referring element, as in (9), or a bound variable, as in (10)).

As mentioned above, when children are presented with a situation where Father Bear washes somebody else, and hear sentence (9), they correctly accept this sentence as a true description of the situation. Grimshaw and Rosen (1990) argue children distinguish between grammatical and ungrammatical structures, which shows their knowledge of the relevant linguistic principles (Principle B in this case). According to these authors, children possess the relevant knowledge, but (sometimes) do not obey it. This failure of obedience is, presumably, due to some problems with experimental designs, and other extralinguistic factors. A detailed discussion of Grimshaw and Rosen's approach can be found in Avrutin and Wexler 1992, and, especially, in Grodzinsky and Reinhart 1993. Here, I want to mention just two questions that are relevant for the current discussion. First, why do children show both knowledge and obedience in reflexive conditions, and second, why does their performance improve in quantificational constructions? Let me now turn to two explanations that specifically address these two questions.

Grodzinsky and Reinhart (1993) offer a processing account of the observed deficit based on the theoretical work of Reinhart (1983, 1986). The central point of Reinhart's approach is that even those pronominals that have an R-expression antecedent can be interpreted as bound variables. The difference between quantificational and non-quantificational constructions is that, in the former case, the interpretation of a pronoun is unambiguously a bound variable, while in the latter case, the pronoun can be either a bound variable or a referring element. The idea (originally due to Sag 1977 and Williams 1977) is that R-expressions can function as quantifiers (the so-called generalised quantifiers). Unlike "real" quantifiers, however, R-expressions function as quantifiers only optionally. In terms of derivations, it amounts to saying that, at LF, "real" quantifiers undergo obligatory raising, while R-expressions do so optionally. (11) and (12) illustrate the point.

(11) Every girl walked her dog. (S-structure)
Every girl t walked her dog (LF)
$\forall x\ (girl(x) \longrightarrow x\ walked\ x's\ dog)$ (Interpretation)
(12) Mary walked her dog. (S-structure)
  a. Mary t walked her dog (LF; *Mary* functions as a generalised quantifier)
  Mary $\lambda_i(x)$ (x_i walked x_i's dog)
  (Interpretation; λ is a functional abstractor)
  b. Mary walked her dog (LF; *Mary* is a regular R-expression)
  Mary walked her dog

  (Interpretation: *her* refers to a singular female individual who happens to be Mary).

Grodzinsky and Reinhart propose Rule I, which is meant to specify when speakers can use (12a) and (12b). A detailed discussion of Rule I can be found in Heim 1992 and Avrutin 1994. Suffice it to say here that Rule I allows reading (12b) (coreference) only if it yields a meaning different from that obtained by a bound variable interpretation (12a). Thus, in this approach, the bound variable anaphora is the center of the dependency relation, while coreference is a marginal case. Principle B of the binding theory applies only to bound variables and rules out sentences where pronouns are locally bound by a coindexed antecedent. The coreference, which in Reinhart's system does not involve coindexation, is ruled out by Rule I. Thus, normal speakers reject (13) because both of its possible representations (bound variable and coreference) are ruled out: the first one by Principle B, and the second one by Rule I.

(13) Father Bear washed him.

Notice that to correctly use Rule I speakers have to figure out whether coreference gives an interpretation different from the bound variable. In order to do that, speakers have to compare the resulting representations to the context, which, according to Grodzinsky and Reinhart, requires additional processing resources. They suggest that children and Broca's aphasics are unable to maintain the two representations (coreferential and bound variable), which results in their being lost. In other words, children and aphasics accept (13) not because of some problems with Principle B, but because of their failure to implement Rule I. This approach correctly predicts that when Rule I does not apply (quantificational constructions, sentences with reflexives), children and aphasics should not have any problems.

One of the appealing characteristics of this analysis, I believe, is that it attempts to provide a unified explanation for the similarities found in children and Broca's aphasics. Indeed, Grodzinsky et al (1993) showed that Broca's (but not Wernicke's) aphasics are also at chance in sentences of type (13), but are significantly above chance in sentences with reflexives, or pronouns bound by quantifiers. There are several problems with this approach, however. First of all, it is not detailed in the sense that there is no proposal of what exactly is missing in these two populations. Clearly, neither children nor aphasics get lost every time they hear a potentially ambiguous structure or word. The question is why they are so sensitive to the bound variable/coreference ambiguity. Moreover, the evidence that Grodzinsky and Reinhart advance to support their processing view is based on a very specific interpretation of Swinney et al's priming experiment (Swinney, Nicol and Zurif 1989, Swinney and Prather 1989). It was shown that children and aphasics show priming only for the most frequent meaning of an ambiguous word, while normal subjects show priming for both meanings. Grodzinsky and Reinhart interpret this result as evidence that these populations cannot processes two representations simultaneously. This view, however, is different from the traditional interpretation of these results, which suggests that the most frequent meaning is accessed first, and that the mechanism responsible for this access is slowed down (at least in aphasia).

But, more importantly, there seems to be empirical evidence that the Rule I approach to the child data is not correct. This evidence comes from Russian subjunctive clauses discussed in Avrutin and Wexler (in press). Briefly, the pronoun in the subject position of a subjunctive clause in Russian cannot be coindexed with the matrix subject. At the same time, reflexive in this position is also ungrammatical, as shown in (14).

(14) *Ivan xočet čtoby on/sebja prygnul.
 Ivan wants that he/himself jumped

Thus, there is no way to use a bound variable representation in this case, which means that children (and aphasics) should not have any problem. In the experiment reported in Avrutin and Wexler (in press), however, Russian speaking children exhibited exactly the same pattern of responses as in other, traditional constructions. Such a result is not predicted in Grodzinsky and Reinhart's theory because, in their view, the problem arises only when there are two competing representations, and subjects are lost while trying to figure out whether one of them is allowed. When there is no ambiguity (as in case of subjunctive constructions), there should be no deficit.

As mentioned above, a different explanation was proposed by Chien and Wexler (1991). The central idea is that children lack certain knowledge that is responsible for the connection between reference and indexation. Chien and Wexler formulate pragmatic Principle P that states that two coreferential NPs are coindexed (unless context specifies otherwise). Thus, for normal adults, if *Father Bear* and *him* in (13) have different indices, they necessarily designate different individuals. This sentence is rejected by normal adults as a description of a situation where Father Bear washed himself because Principle P requires a coindexation, and Principle B rules it out. Children, it is claimed, lack the knowledge of Principle P, and, therefore, they allow the two NPs in (13) to have different indices, and yet to corefer. Chien and Wexler argue for a highly modular character of the development: the syntactic part of the dependency relation is innate (Principles A and B), while the pragmatic part (Principle P) is acquired some time after the age of six. Presence of the syntactic knowledge is manifested in children's correct responses to reflexive conditions and sentences with quantified antecedents (in this case Principle P is irrelevant because the only way to link a pronoun with a quantifier is by coindexation).

This theory provides an important insight into the relationship between indexation and reference, and the development of this relationship. It is interesting, however, that Broca's aphasics demonstrate a similar pattern of responses. Although it is logically possible that these people lose (as a result of brain damage) some relevant knowledge, it seems to me more plausible that the similarities between children and aphasics have a common explanation in terms of some limitations on processing resources, which is due in the case of aphasics to a brain injury and in the case of children to the non-fully matured brain structures.

Although the indices/reference approach appears to be on the right track, several questions remain unanswered. Given that the problem lies in the interpretation of indices and its relation to reference, the following questions arise:

- What is indexation?
- What is its relation to reference?
- Assuming that children's and aphasics' processing resources are limited, how does this limitation show up in the interpretation of indices, i.e. in their relationship to reference?

The goal of the next three chapters of this book is to develop a model that shows how limitations on computational resources may result in an incorrect interpretation of indices. In order to do that, we first need a theory of indexation and interpretation of indices, a theory that would explain the role indices play in the syntax-discourse interface.

CHAPTER II

SYNTAX, DISCOURSE AND INTERPRETATION OF
PRONOMINALS

In this chapter, I present a model of the syntax-discourse interface. First, I discuss the role indices play in establishing a relevant interpretation of NPs. I show that coindexation of two NPs can either represent variable binding, or *identity of guises for a given referent*. Although these two interpretations are different with respect to the character of elements they apply to, they both establish a dependency relation. In the first case, it is a syntactic dependency, in the second, it is a discourse-related dependency.

I also discuss various ways of introducing an NP into discourse. First, I present a model known as File Change Semantics (Heim 1982). I discuss three mechanisms: Incorporation, Accommodation and Deictic use of an NP. I further develop the existing discourse model and argue that the deictic use of a definite NP is just another case of Accommodation. This proposal will be shown to have important consequences with respect to analyses of children's and aphasics' interpretation of pronouns.

1. General Model

When speakers take part in a conversation, they use various aspects of their knowledge. Speakers, clearly, have to know words of their language (i.e. to possess lexical knowledge). They must be able to combine words into grammatical strings (i.e. to possess syntactic competence), and to combine these strings (sentences) into a coherent text (i.e. to possess knowledge of some discourse rules and strategies).

CHAPTER II

To make a conversation mutually understandable and informative, speakers must also share some world knowledge, roughly speaking, they must know what they are talking about. The following simplified model illustrates relationship between these domains of knowledge.

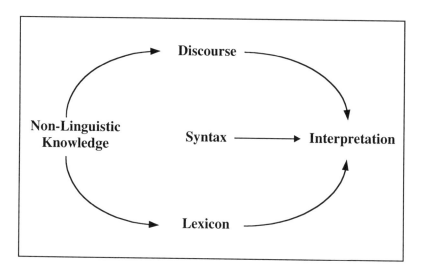

To be able to correctly interpret sentences, speakers must be able to combine the lexical, syntactic and discourse-related knowledge. They, clearly, must know the meaning of the words. They must be able to represent the syntactic structure of the sentence, for example to know who did what to whom in a sentence "Mary showed John Bill". They also must know some rules of the discourse to correctly interpret *he* as *John* in "John came home late after drinking with Bill. He was tired". Thus, interpretation of sentences requires an integration of different types of knowledge.

Consider, for example, a noun *dog*. Suppose a speaker wants to say something about a dog. He or she pulls out of the lexicon the lexical item *dog*, which is inserted into the syntactic tree. In the output of syntax, we have a phrase that carries some lexical and syntactic information: [NP a dog], or [NP the dog]. This NP is presented to the discourse where it is subject to some new, discourse-related mechanisms. The questions now are: what are these mechanisms, and what is the discourse representation of NPs? The second question is of particular interest because it is directly relevant to the question of how NPs are interpreted. The discourse representation of a NP, in turn, depends on what kind of NP it is. Syntactically, NPs can be either definite, or indefinite, and definite NPs can be either 'names' (or, rather, 'R-expressions' as in Chomsky 1986), or pronominals (pronouns, reflexives; I put aside quantifiers for a moment).

I begin with a brief summary of the syntactic conditions that are commonly accepted to be responsible for the distribution of pronouns and reflexives. Then, I show that in those cases where pronominals (specifically pronouns) are interpreted through discourse, their distribution can be best analysed if we abstract away (at least in part) from their pronominal nature, and focus on the fact that they are definite NPs. Let us begin with the following questions about pronouns: how are these elements interpreted, and what kind of syntactic and non-syntactic principles are involved in their interpretation?

2. Syntactic Constraints and Interpretation of Indices

From the traditional syntactic point of view, the principles regulating distribution of pronouns and reflexives appear to be straightforward. These principles are known in the literature as Principles A and B of the Binding Theory. Stated somewhat informally, these principles are repeated below (for a more detailed discussion see, for example, Lasnik 1989):

Principle A: Reflexives must be locally bound.

Principle B: Pronouns must be locally free.

Locality in these conditions is defined in structural terms (for example, a clause), and binding is defined as c-commanding and coindexation. Thus, only (1) below violates Principle B:

(1) *Mary$_i$ likes her$_i$.

(2) Mary's$_i$ father likes her$_i$.

(3) [Mary$_i$ thinks [John likes her$_i$]].

The pronoun *her* in (1) is in local c-commanding relation with its antecedent, thus the sentence is ruled out. In (2), although the pronoun is, in some sense, local to its antecedent, there is no c-commanding relation between them, hence no binding. And in (3), although *Mary* does c-command *her*, the pronoun is sufficiently far away from its antecedent, therefore *her* can be interpreted as *Mary*.

While the notions of c-command and locality are unproblematic in that they can be defined in structural terms, the notion of coindexation is less transparent. The first, intuitive, view on coindexation is that it represents coreference. That is, in (3) *Mary* refers to a certain person named *Mary* (or, rather, to the speaker's mental representation of this person), and *her* also refers to this person. Thus, the two NPs are coreferential, and, therefore, coindexed.

There are two problems with equating coindexation and coreference. First, in sentences with quantified antecedents, it is meaningless to talk about coreference simply because pronouns (and their antecedents) have no reference:

(4) [Every boy]$_i$ thinks he$_i$ is smart.

Since quantifiers do not refer, the pronoun *he* in (4) cannot be said to be coreferential with its antecedent. Rather, it is interpreted in this case as a variable bound by an operator, that is its value is determined by the value picked by the universal quantifier *every* from a pre-established set of boys. Thus, although *every boy* and *he* are coindexed, this coindexation clearly does not represent coreference.

The second problem arises if we consider some 'marginal' cases, that is sentences which should be ruled out by (the orthodox version of)

Principle B. These sentences, exemplified below, have attracted significant attention from both linguists and philosophers of language (e.g. Higginbotham 1985, Reinhart 1983, Heim 1993, among others). The most recent analyses of pronominal interpretation in these constructions are provided in Heim 1993, which I will discuss briefly.[2]

(5) -- Who is this speaker?

    -- It must be Zelda. She praises her to the sky. No other candidate would do it.

(6) Everybody hates Lucifer. Only he himself pities him.

(7) You know what Mary, Sue and John have in common? Mary admires John, Sue admires him, and John admires him, too.

(8) That must be John. At least, he looks like him.

(from Chien and Wexler 1990)

Consider, for example, (5), specifically the sentence 'She praises her to the sky'. Both *she* and *her* refer to the same individual named Zelda, in fact there is only one individual around, or, at least under, consideration. Thus, *she* and *her* are coreferential in the sense that they have a common referent. But if coreference implies coindexation, *she* and *her* in this sentence should be coindexed, and the sentence should be ruled out as a violation of Principle B. Still, (5) is perfectly acceptable. The same holds for examples (6) - (8).

A conclusion that we can draw from these examples (and from quantificational constructions) is that coindexation does not, in fact, represent coreference, but has some other interpretation. To see what could be said more plausibly about coindexation, recall the distinction between *Sense* and *Reference* introduced by Goettlibe Frege (Frege 1892). Frege suggested that two different terms, for example *Morning Star* and *Evening Star,* may have the same reference but different senses. In the morning, or in the evening, when speakers talk about some bright star in the sky, they actually talk about Planet Venus, which is the same in the morning, and in the evening. Thus, in Fregian terms, both Morning Star and Evening Star have the same reference. In the context of their conversation, however, Planet Venus discussed in the morning is represented differently from Planet Venus discussed in the evening. The two terms, thus, have different senses, where sense is a context-dependent notion for some referent. Crucially, one and the same referent may have different senses, provided there are appropriate contextual conditions that introduce these different senses for the same referent. In the absence of such conditions, one and the same referent appears in discourse as having one and the same sense. For example, astronomers observing Venus in the telescope and discussing its motion, represent it in their conversation as one and the same object observable at different times of the day. In their conversation, the thing they observe in the morning has the same sense and reference as the thing they observe in the evening.

What do these ideas have to do with indices? Let us look again at the sentences above, for example (5). Notice that when the middle sentence appears in isolation, with no surrounding context as in (9), this sentence is actually ruled out:

(9) *She$_i$ praises her$_i$.

As Heim (1993) points out, the difference between the two cases is that in (5), one and the same person (referent) Zelda appears under two different guises. One guise is provided through the speaker's visual context (pointing to the speaker), and the other is something like our memory entry regarding Zelda. Of course, some special contextual conditions are necessary, which are provided through discourse. Indeed, when the discourse is not there, as in (9), there is no evidence that one person (one referent) has two different guises (senses). In (9), the sense and reference of Zelda coincide, while in (5) the context disambiguates between them. And it is not a coincidence that only (5), but not (9) is grammatical. Following Heim's proposal[3], we say that in (5), *she* and *her* are not, actually, coindexed, while they are in (9). They bear different indices in (5) because the context here provides different guises for the same referent. In other words, the index denotes the guise, not the referent of the NP; that is, it denotes the way a particular object is introduced in the discourse. Coindexation, therefore, represents the identity of guises, not the identity of referents.

The two pronouns in (5), therefore, will bear different indices, as in (10).

-- Who is this speaker?
-- It must be Zelda. She$_i$ praises her$_j$ to the sky. No other candidate would do it.

The reasoning of the person uttering (10) can be paraphrased as something like this: "I know that there is one person, Zelda, who is running for presidency. But here I see a speaker [one guise] who talks about the best candidate [second guise]. Pronouns *she* and *her* therefore will refer to different guises (hence, will not be coindexed). The sentence is syntactically well-formed, and, moreover, satisfies discourse conditions: I am introducing two file cards for the same referent because there is a good reason for this – the referent is represented under two different guises." The listener, accordingly, will be able to infer that the person who utters (10) has introduced a new file card in order to identify a new guise for Zelda. In the absence of context, as in (9), there is no evidence that one and the same referent appears under two different guises, therefore *she* and *her* are coindexed. The point is that the distinction between *sense* and *reference* noticed by philosophers is reflected in natural languages by means of the indexation mechanism.

Let us now return to quantificational constructions:

(11) [Every boy]$_i$ thinks he$_i$ is smart.

Given that quantifiers (and bound variables) do not have reference, and therefore cannot denote guises of their referents, we have to say something about what coindexing represents in (11).

It has been argued in the literature (most notably in Reinhart 1983, 1986) that the coindexation exemplified in (11) is the only meaningful type of coindexation. Reinhart argues that the only interpretation of coindexation is variable binding familiar from formal logic. Thus, (11) receives the following interpretation:

(12) $\forall x \, (boy(x) \longrightarrow x \text{ thinks that } x \text{ is smart})$.

Referring expressions in this theory do not have any indices, and their interpretation is achieved by some discourse mechanisms, which indexation has nothing to do with. For example, in (13) neither *John*, nor *he* has any index:[4]

(13) John's mother thinks that he is smart.

John is interpreted as referring to some person John mentioned in the previous discourse, and *he* is interpreted as a single male individual referring to some entity also introduced in the discourse, and which also happens to be John. In other words, indexation is a purely syntactic mechanism that has nothing to do with discourse, or, for that matter, reference.

Notice, however, that both bound variable anaphora (as in (11)), and discourse anaphora (as in (13)) are types of dependency relation. They are different in nature, of course, but the difference lies in *the level* of application, rather than in the character of the relation. Variable binding is a dependency relation established *at the level of syntax*, while the other type of dependency is established *at the discourse level*.

I suggest that we can use one mechanism (indexation) to express both types of dependency, and that the difference between the types lies in the interpretation of indices.[5] Before making this proposal, however, we need to have a model of discourse. Then, we will be able to ask the question of what role indices (and coindexation) play in this model, that is how coindexation is represented at the level of discourse, and whether it is possible to use one and the same mechanism (indices) to represent two different types of dependencies. In what follows, I present one of the existing models of discourse, which is known as File Change Semantics, and then make a specific proposal regarding the interpretation of indices by normal adults, children and Broca's aphasics.

3. File Change Semantics

File Change Semantics is a discourse model originally proposed in Heim 1982. The intuitive idea behind this model is that the goal of a conversation is to convey some information from one participant to the other. The second participant (the listener) keeps track of this information by creating file cards and updating information on them, similar to record keeping in a library's file catalogue. Consider, for example, the following conversation (from Heim 1982). There are two participants in the conversation: A and B. A utters sentences (14), and B extracts the information, and keeps a record of it.

(14) a) A woman was bitten by a dog.
    b) She hit him with a paddle.
    c) It broke in half.
    d) The dog ran away.

The file change proceeds in the following way. After sentence (a), B takes two new cards and gives each a number (1 and 2). On card 1, B writes:

> 1: "is a woman"; "was bitten by 2"

On card 2, B writes:

> 2: "is a dog"; "bit 1"

After sentence (b), B takes a new card, gives it a number (3), and writes:

> 3: "is a paddle; was used by 1 to hit 2"

Speaker B at this moment also updates the information on card 1, that is two new entries are added: "hit 2 with 3" (on card 1) and "was hit by 1 with 3" (on card 2).

After (c), speaker B updates card (3):

> 3: "broke in half"

Finally, after hearing sentence (d), the speaker updates card (2):

2: "ran away"

Each indefinite NP that appears in the discourse requires introduction of a new file card, that is a card with a new number. Definite NPs do not introduce new cards, rather information on an existing card is updated. Second, different file cards do not necessarily correspond to different referents. Two different cards can, in fact, have one and the same referent. *File cards correspond to the way this referent is presented in the discourse*, or, using Heim's terminology, they introduce *guises*. Thus, as discussed above, in example (10), *she* and *her* represent different guises of the same referent (Zelda). A different guise is associated with a different file card, and a different file card is associated with a different number in the file catalogue. Let us now return to the original question of interpretation of indices on referring and non-referring elements, more specifically to the relation between NPs, their indices, file cards and their numbers.

4. Interpretation of Indices in Syntax and Discourse

Pronouns can be interpreted either as bound variables, or as referring elements. These two types of dependency are known as *bound variable anaphora* and *coreference*. I suggested above that we can use one mechanism (indexation) to express both types of dependency, and that the difference between the two types lies in the interpretation of indices. Contrary to Reinhart (1983, 1986) who claims that indices are optionally assigned to NPs, let us suppose that nouns come from the lexicon with an index. This is, of course, similar to Heim's (1993) proposal where she stipulates that all pronouns come from the lexicon with an index. I suggest that this is not a stipulation. What comes from the lexicon is an element (let's say *dog*) that has a specific syntactic property (+N). This element is inserted into syntactic structure where it projects a full NP. Notice that a noun does not denote any particular individual, but a set (in the case of *dog*, for example, it denotes a set of all possible dogs.) In this sense *dog* is a variable whose value ranges over all possible dogs. *Dog*, however, is just a lexical item, so it is better to say that it carries a variable index whose value ranges over all possible individuals of the set denoted by this item. The index of *dog*, for example, ranges over all possible dogs and the index of *table* ranges over all possible tables. Having a variable index, therefore, is an inherent property of elements that denote sets -- nouns in particular[6].

Following traditional assumptions, we can say that the index of an NP is the same as the index of its head. This can be described as an index percolation, or it may follow from the X-bar theory. What is important is that the index of an NP, therefore, is also a variable. But this is somewhat counterintuitive. Indeed, while it is intuitively plausible that *dog* does not denote any particular individual, NP *the dog*, or *a dog* is interpreted by speakers as denoting a single representative of the set of dogs. Such an interpretation would not be surprising if the index of an NP was a constant (some number), not a variable. The question is why we are able to use NPs to talk about individuals, although the indices on NPs are variables.

A straightforward answer to this question is that by the time an NP is interpreted, its index is no longer a variable, but a constant. Recall now that we are dealing with constants at the level of discourse representation as well: file cards that represent NPs have numbers, and numbers are constants. Suppose then that we interpret NPs as denoting individuals because the syntax-discourse interface can be characterised as **instantiation of a variable (index) with a constant (number of a file card)**. The set of rules is presented below. The first two rules correspond to what was proposed in Heim (1982): an Indefinite NP introduces a new file card, a definite NP does not. The third rule says that NP_i and NP_i will be represented by the same file card (the same index will be instantiated with the same number), and NP_i and NP_j will be represented by two different cards (two different instantiating numbers).

> **Rules of NP Representation in Discourse**
>
> 1. **Instantiate the variable index of an Indefinite NP with a number of a new file card.**
>
> 2. **Instantiate the variable index of a definite NP with a number of an old file card.**
>
> 3. **Instantiate two identical variable indices with the same number, and two different indices with different numbers.**

In syntax, NP *a/the dog* has a variable index. By Rule 1 or 2, this index is instantiated by the number of a new card, or an old one (say, card #7). Thus, speakers interpret *a/the dog* as denoting an individual because the representation that is actually interpreted is something like DOG #7, not $[_{NP}$ the dog$]_i$. The latter is its syntactic representation, but interpretation of NPs operates on their discourse representation. Why can't we say that the syntactic representation of an NP can be an input to its interpretation? After all, syntax does directly contribute to the interpretation of a sentence. The answer is two-fold. First, as discussed above, discourse plays a crucial role in establishing reference for NPs, pronouns in particular. Sentences of type (10) illustrate the point. A different indexation for *she* and *her* is possible only because the discourse supplies different guises for one and the same referent, thus making the sentence grammatical with respect to Principle B. The second reason is that sentences with free (unbound) variables are not interpretable.

It follows then that (in the absence of any operator that binds the variables in syntax), variable indices must be instantiated. In other words, indices of NPs (variables) must be translated into numbers of file cards (constants). Thus, only the discourse representation of NP *a/the dog* can function as an input to interpretation, and only in this case this NP will be interpreted as denoting an individual dog.

It also follows that an NP with a bound index can be interpreted. This is the case of quantifiers and bound variables. Consider, for example, (15).

(15) Every boy$_i$ thinks he$_i$ is smart.

The noun *boy* and pronoun *he* (which functions as a definite NP) come from the lexicon with an index. Let us suppose they have the same indices. These indices are bound in syntax (at LF) by the universal quantifier *every*. Thus, the sentence contains no free variables, and it can be interpreted as in (16).

(16) $\forall x_i$ (boy(x_i) ---> x_i thinks x_i is smart)

As expected, quantifiers and bound variables do not denote individuals, but rather sets. This is predicted because their indices are variables, not constants. In other words, the requirement of interpretability is satisfied in this case by binding variables, not by instantiating them. Moreover, this is the only possible way of satisfying this constraint because the operator-variable relation (requiring coindexation) is established at LF. For definite and indefinite NPs it is their discourse representation that is interpreted, while for quantifiers, it is their syntactic representation.

Recall now (5) repeated below as (17).
-- Who is this speaker?
-- It must be Zelda. She praises her to the sky. No other candidate would do it.

As argued above, *she* and *her* have different indices because the discourse provides different guises for the same referent, that is the discourse allows introduction of two different cards for *she* and *her*. But if quantifiers are not represented by file cards, we predict that a quantificational construction corresponding to (17) is ungrammatical. This is the case, as (18) demonstrates.

(18) Who are these speakers? It must be Zelda, Mary and Jane.
 *Every one praises her to the sky. None of the other candidates would do it.

The coindexation of *each of them* and *her* is prohibited by Principle B. And since quantifiers are not represented by file cards, they cannot represent any guise of some referent, which was possible in (17). Thus, (18) is ungrammatical.

Consider now (19).

(19) The speaker praised her.

The speaker, as a definite NP, has a variable index i, which is instantiated with some file card number, say #9. The pronoun *her* cannot be generated with the same index due to Principle B. But, as a definite NP, it must have some index, so it receives a different index, say j. According to Rule 3, this index is instantiated with a different number, say #5. The only interpretation of this representation is such that NP *the speaker* represents a guise of some individual introduced into the discourse by file card #9 and *her* represents a guise of some female individual represented by file card #5. In the absence of any discourse, this means that the speaker praised some other female person. If the appropriate discourse is present, however, this can also mean that one and the same person presented under two different guises praises herself. This is the case of (10) discussed above.

Notice that there is an implicit "markedness" assumption regarding the relationship of a referent to a guise. The idea is that the default, unmarked case for a discourse representation of a referent is that different guises represent different referents. It is only when the context provides some additional, marked conditions that one and the same referent is allowed to be represented by different guises (file cards). This assumption was already evident in the Chien and Wexler's (1990) proposal regarding the relationship between reference and indexation, which they formulated as Principle P (see also Avrutin and Wexler 1992).

Principle P: Two coreferential elements are coindexed unless the context specifies otherwise.

In the proposed framework, such an assumption seems to be quite plausible and based on economy considerations. Indeed, the smaller the file (that is, the fewer cards it contains), the easier it is to maintain it (that is, keep record). It is plausible, therefore, that the economy (information-processing) considerations result in the following constraint on file change:

(20) Avoid introduction of new file cards, unless it is required by syntax and/or discourse.

This is, essentially, a reformulation of Chien and Wexler's proposal, but with more psycholinguistic flavour. Clearly, the notion of economy comes into play from the speaker's side: He/she is the one who follows this constraint while uttering sentences. It is important, however, that the listener assumes that the speaker follows the economy considerations. The situation is exactly the same as in other cases of communication. Consider, for instance, a classical Gricean example. If someone says that John has one leg, it is, strictly speaking, true even if John has two legs. But the listener will infer from this statement that John actually has only one leg. This is so because the listener assumes that the speaker follows certain rules of conversation and, under normal circumstances, will provide just the right amount of information. In the case of (20), too, the listener can make inferences about the "normal", economical way of file keeping. And, returning now to our example (19), we can see why *the speaker* and *her* have different references: they are represented by two different file cards, which (as follows from the constraint on file change introduced above) is a way of representing two, not one, referents.

Let me clarify the constraint on the introduction of new file cards. The crucial part of (20) is that a new file card can (and must) be introduced if it is required by syntax and/or discourse. From the syntactic part of the system, a new file card may be required, for example, if a syntactic violation would arise otherwise. This is the case of (9) when the two pronouns must bear different indices (to avoid

Principle B violation) and, therefore, they must be represented by two different cards. But an introduction of a new file card may also be required by discourse conditions. For example, as discussed above, one referent is normally represented by one file card (following (20)). But given a specific context, as in (10), a new file card may be required because of the contextual, non-syntactic reasons.

As stated in Rule 2, indices on definite NPs are instantiated by numbers of previously existing cards. In other words, a definite NP can, apparently, be used only if there was a previous mention of this NP (either in its definite or indefinite form: all that is required is that there is a previously established file card). In the following section, I show that this does not have always to be the case. There are cases where speakers (apparently) violate this rule. I argue that, in fact, no violation, but a modification of this rule is in order.

5. Various Uses of Definite NPs

The question of how and when speakers use definite NPs is one of the most widely discussed questions in the philosophical, psychological and psycholinguistic literature.[7] The reason for this interest is that definites are extensively used by speakers in a variety of contexts, but a more or less precise characteristic of these uses is extremely difficult to achieve.

On the face of it, the situation appears to be quite simple. When an NP is used in a conversation for the first time, this NP has to be indefinite. Afterwards, a corresponding definite NP can be used to refer to the previously established referent (that is, the referent established by the use of the indefinite NP). This simple case is exemplified in (21).

(21) I saw a cat. The cat/ he was hungry.

It is infelicitous to use a definite NP without establishing an appropriate reference:

(22) #The cat/he was hungry.

The situation, however, is much more complex. In many cases, speakers introduce a definite NP without ever mentioning any antecedent, but the sentence still sounds perfectly normal. Here are several examples taken from Heim 1982 and Hawkins 1978. As I am walking up a driveway, someone says to me:

(23) Watch out, the dog will bite you!

There was no previous mention of a dog, and there is no reason to assume that I know which dog we are talking about, or, for that matter, that this dog exists. Still, this, so-called Immediate Situation Use of a definite NP is perfectly natural. Another example is the so-called Larger Situation Use:

(24) The sun is shining.

Speakers do not have to say: "There is a sun. The Sun is shining". This first mention of the definite NP *the Sun* is natural, as well as in (25) below:

(25) I wonder where the City Hall is.

Although there was no mention of a city hall before, this is a pragmatically normal question in a new town. Interestingly, this use depends on some shared knowledge, or at least on the assumption that some relevant knowledge is shared both by the speaker, and the listener. More specifically, it is assumed that this knowledge is shared by members of a certain community, and the size of this community may vary. In (24), the community is the population of the planet Earth, which has only one sun. Thus, for this population, the first mention of the definite NP *the Sun* uniquely identifies the referent. In (25), the shared knowledge is some knowledge about the political system in the US, thus this sentence is felicitous for members of the American community. And the correct identification of the referent in (26) is possible for an even smaller group of people all of whom possess certain knowledge about who the boss is:

(26) You know, Mary met the boss yesterday in a local pub.

One of the most interesting examples of the first mention use of a definite NP is the so-called associative anaphoric use, as in (27).

(27) John read a book about Dali and wrote to the author.

No author has ever been mentioned in the previous discourse, but the definite NP is quite appropriate. Moreover, it is necessarily interpreted as referring to the author of the book mentioned in the previous clause. This use is very interesting because it requires making certain inferences on the basis of non-linguistic knowledge. That is, we have to know that books, normally, have authors. Other examples require some knowledge of the physical world, for example:

(28) I bought a couch recently that wouldn't fit into the elevator. The length was too big. The colour really pleased me, but the weight displeased Kevin and Danny.

In (29), the use of a definite NP appears to be possible on a basis of our knowledge of some social conventions:

(29) I attended a wedding recently. The bride was wearing a white dress.

Intuitively, what is happening here is that the first (indefinite) NP serves as a trigger for some associations, for example:[8]

wedding: bride, music, cake, etc.
couch: length, weight, colour, etc.

It is not the case, of course, that this kind of connection between NPs in discourse (based on the triggering) is always possible. Clearly, certain conditions have to be satisfied that would account for the fact that (31) sounds more coherent that (30).

(30) The man drove by in a big car. The dog was barking furiously.
(31) The man drove by in a big car. The exhaust fumes were terrible.

It appears that *car* can trigger *the exhaust fumes* more naturally than it can trigger *the dog*. The possibility of triggering is interesting because it tells us something about how our knowledge is organised.

There are many more examples, of course, but these sentences illustrate the point I want to make. It is not necessary to have a linguistically mentioned antecedent to use a definite NP. At the same time, it is not the case, of course, that speakers can use definite NPs whenever they want. There are some restrictions, that is, some conditions do exist that license the use of a definite NP without any previous mention of its antecedent. And the associative anaphoric use is not always possible, at least in many cases it requires some additional effort. For example, if a speaker utters (32), the listener will have to assume that there is some contextual connection between the book and the girl (e.g. the girl had asked me to do so a long time ago.) This is so because the listener, under normal circumstances, assumes that the speaker participates in a rational conversation.

(32) ?I bought a book. The little girl was happy.
(33) I bought a book. The author was well-known to me.

No such effort is required in (33), as, presumably, all participants in the conversation know that books have authors. This knowledge, of course, is culture specific: If the listener belongs to a culture where books do not have authors (or, the listener *does not know* that they do,) (33) will be pragmatically infelicitous. The speaker in this case cannot utter (33) if he/she intends to maintain a normal conversation.

In terms of file change semantics, these examples show that under certain circumstances a definite NP can introduce a new file card, that is it can receive a new index. This observation is particularly important for analyses of pronouns. This is so because a pronoun cannot be c-commanded by another (local) NP *only if it has the same index*. Now, if definite NPs (including pronouns) can, in some cases, be represented in discourse by a new file card, which means that they can, in some cases, receive a new index, we want to know the mechanisms of introducing new file cards for definite NPs, and conditions when such an introduction becomes possible.

To summarise, NPs are represented in discourse by file cards. A file card can be either an already existing one, or a new one. What are the ways of associating an NP with a file card? According to Heim 1982, there are two possibilities: Incorporation and Accommodation.

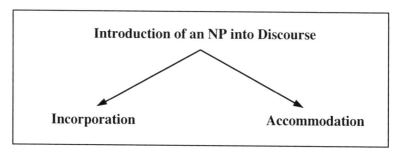

Incorporation is a procedure of updating information on an already existing file card, that is adding some new entries. Accommodation is a procedure that is carried by so-called Inferential Bridging (Clark 1977, Clark and Marshall 1981). Let us consider these two mechanisms in some detail.

6. Incorporation and Accommodation

Consider first some examples of Incorporation.

(34) I saw a cat. The cat was hungry.

A cat is an indefinite NP. Therefore, its index is instantiated with the number of a new file card, say #1. *The cat*, on the other hand, is a definite NP. It has an index that has to be instantiated with a number of some existing file card. In order to do this, this NP looks for a file card that has an entry IS A CAT. This card is updated, i.e. it receives an additional entry: IS HUNGRY. As a result of this operation, at the level of discourse representation, there is one card with two entries:

```
1:   IS A CAT

     IS HUNGRY
```

Consider another example, this time with a pronoun:

(35) I met a boy named Bill, and I met a girl named Mary. I introduced Bill to Mary. He was very happy.

By the end of the second sentence, we have two different cards:

```
4: IS A BOY

   IS NAMED BILL
```

```
5: IS A GIRL

   IS NAMED MARY
```

Now, *he* has an index that has to be instantiated. It looks for a card that matches its description, that is a card that has the following entry: IS A SINGLE MALE INDIVIDUAL. It cannot be associated with *Mary*; in fact, in this file there is only one candidate, *Bill*. So the index of the pronoun is instantiated with #4 and the card gets updated:

HE: IS A SINGLE MALE INDIVIDUAL.

```
4:  IS A BOY

    IS NAMED BILL

    IS HAPPY
```

Notice that the operation of incorporation, as shown here, is, in a sense, automatic. We just look for relevant entries on the file cards, which are, in turn, part of lexical meaning. No inferences are necessary for this operation.

What happens in cases like (35)?

(35) I attended a wedding recently. The bride was wearing a white dress.

NP *a wedding* is represented by a new card (because it is indefinite), e.g. #8:

> 8: IS A WEDDING

What about *the bride*? Although there is no syntactic prohibition, this NP cannot have the same index as *a wedding*. This is because, according to Rule 3, its index would have to be instantiated by the card number representing *a wedding,* and the information on this card would have to be updated in the following way:

> 8: IS A WEDDING
>
> IS WEARING A WHITE DRESS

This is, of course, a nonsense card. Roughly speaking, incorporation leads to identity, which is not the case here. Thus, *the bride* cannot have the same index as *a wedding*. At the same time, according to Rule 2, its index has to be instantiated by the number of some previously existing card. Thus, Rule 2 has to be modified in a certain way to allow for the so-called *accommodation by bridging*.

What it means is that a definite NP can (under certain conditions) introduce a new file card, but this card has to be 'bridged' with a previously existing one. There can be no accommodation without bridging. The index of NP *the bride* is instantiated by some new number, say 10, and it is represented in discourse as:

> 10: IS A BRIDE of (8)

Thus, the representation of definite NPs that are accommodated is different from the representation of incorporated definite NPs in that accommodated NPs are represented by a new file card with a new number.

As mentioned above, bridging is an operation that requires some inferences, and these inferences are based on our world knowledge that we share with other speakers. For example, our knowledge tells us that a wedding implies the presence of a bride; therefore, we can build an inferential bridge between the two cards with different numbers. In this case, it is our cultural knowledge. In other cases, bridging becomes possible due to some very specific knowledge shared by a small group of people, as in (36):

(36) I went to a presentation last Tuesday. The food was good.

Bridging is only possible for some small group of people because they share some knowledge about free lunch served at these presentations.

These examples show that another rule has to be added to the three rules listed in Section 4, a rule that would allow for the cases of accommodation. The rules are listed below.

Rules of NP Representation in Discourse

1. **Instantiate the variable index of an Indefinite NP with a number of a new file card.**

2. **Instantiate the variable index of a definite NP with a number of an old file card.**

3. **Instantiate two identical variable indices with the same number, and two different indices with different numbers.**

4. **Instantiate the variable index of a definite NP with a number of a new file card only if this card can be bridged to another one.**

Notice that from the discourse point of view, definite NPs are "deficient": their file cards cannot stand on their own. They require some kind of referential support -- either in the form of incorporation, or bridging.

Now let us return for a moment to the claim that quantifiers and bound variables are not represented by file cards. Interestingly, bridging provides additional evidence for this claim. As discussed above, bridging is an operation that takes place at the level of discourse, that is at the level of file cards. Thus, the prediction is that if an NP is not represented by a file card, no bridging will be possible. Examples below show that this is the case.

(37) a. John read a book and wrote to the author.
b. *John read every book in the library and wrote the author.

In (37a), speakers can use a definite NP *the author* because the file card that represents this NP can be bridged to the card representing *a book*. But in (37b), this becomes impossible: quantifiers are not represented by file cards, and, therefore, no bridging is possible. Another example is based on Heim's (1982) analyses of indefinite NPs in the so-called "donkey-anaphora" sentences. Heim argues that the indefinite NP *a donkey* in (38) is interpreted as a variable.

(38) Every farmer who owns a donkey beats it.

A detailed analyses of these sentences can be found in Heim (1982). Suffice it to say that *a donkey* is interpreted as a variable which is bound in syntax (at LF). For the current discussion it is important that this NP is not represented by a file card because it is interpreted as a bound variable. By contrast, in (39), *a donkey* is not a variable and, therefore, has a corresponding file card.

(39) John, who owns a donkey, beats it.

The prediction, thus, is that the bridging with an indefinite NP should be possible in (39), but not in (38). This prediction is borne out, as examples (40a,b) demonstrate.

(40) a. John, who has recently read a book, burnt it. The author was mad.
b. *Every student who has recently read a book burned it. The author was mad.

Only in (40a) is the bridging possible because only in this case does the indefinite NP have a corresponding file card, which the card representing the definite NP could be bridged to.

Let us return now to our discussion of accommodation. As mentioned above, there is no accommodation without bridging. This means that a definite NP cannot introduce a new file card (and, therefore, receive a new index) if it cannot be bridged to some previously existing card. But what happens in cases of no linguistic antecedent, for example (41a,b,c)?

(41) a. I wonder where the city hall is (in a new town).
b. The sun is shining.
c. I like this cat (pointing).

(41a) is an example of the so-called "Immediate Situation Use", (41b) is an example of the "Larger Situation Use", and (41c) is an example of a deictic use of a definite NP.

There are several questions regarding these uses of definite NPs. First, as suggested above, new file cards that introduce definite NPs must be bridged to some existing cards. The question is what the cards introduced in (41a,b,c) are bridged to. The second question is whether these three uses are really different with respect to the discourse representation of the definite NPs. Somewhat developing ideas of Hawkins (1978) and Heim (1982), I suggest that all the three uses of a definite NP are essentially the same. They are the same because in all cases a definite NP is bridged to the so-called Situation Card.

The idea is that speakers never begin a conversation with a completely empty file. There is always some common knowledge regarding the place and time of the conversation, as well as some encyclopaedic knowledge about the world (Ariel 1990). In terms of file change semantics, we can say that there is an initial file card that contains at least some of the relevant information. For convenience, let us assume that this initial card contains several "smaller" cards, each of which corresponds to some situation: for example, the country, the town, the university, etc. So this card looks something like this:

(42)
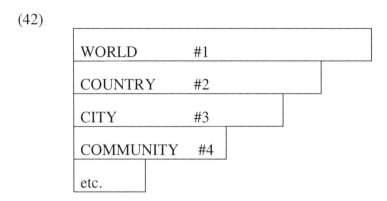

Now, I also assume that each of these cards has its own number (index). This assumption is not crucial, although it will make the story easier. We can now see what happens in (41a) and (41b). The NPs *the town hall* and *the Sun* introduce new file cards which are bridged to the corresponding Situation Cards. *The Sun* is bridged to card #1 (corresponding to the world), and *the town hall* is bridged to card #3 (corresponding to the city where the conversation is taking place). In this sense, this bridging is no different from the bridging of *the bride* to *a wedding*. In all cases, the interpretation is that the new card is related to the old one (the bride of this particular wedding; the town hall of this particular city, etc.).

The question, however, remains regarding the discourse representation of a deictic NP. I propose that this representation is also essentially the same. The idea is that, in the course of a conversation, speakers may introduce an additional card inside the Situation Card, which we may call the Visual Situation Card[9].

(43)

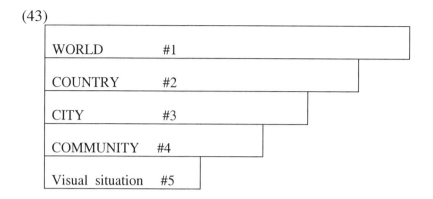

The visual situation surrounding speakers is not something invariable, in fact, it constantly changes. Thus, this situation cannot be represented in the initial setting of the file because the content of the initial situation card reflects some stable knowledge shared by the speakers. But, in principle, it is as legitimate for speakers to make use of their knowledge of what they see NOW, as of their knowledge of what they know ALWAYS. For example, my knowledge that there are food trucks on campus allows me to utter sentences like: "I'm going to the trucks". But for someone who is not aware of these trucks, it is still possible to point to these trucks, and utter the same sentence. The only difference between me and the other speaker is that I do not introduce any new situation cards when I utter this sentence, while the other speaker does. His or her file is changed not only by introducing a new card for *the trucks*, but also by introducing a new Visual Situation Card bridged to the card representing NP *the trucks*. The interpretation of a deictic NP, then, is something like: "The trucks of the visual scene", or, when pointing to a cat, "The cat of the visual scene", etc. Such an interpretation is no different from the ones I discussed for Immediate and Larger Situation Uses, and for the Associative Use. Speakers can talk about the bride (at a wedding), the town hall (of the city), the Sun (of the world). In all cases, there is a bridging between a new card and an old one; the only difference is whether the old one is a permanently present card reflecting some constant knowledge, or a new card introduced for a particular visual situation.

There is an important difference, of course. The deictic use of a definite NP must be accompanied by pointing. In the next section, I show why it is necessary.

7. Constraints on Bridging

To be able to participate in a conversation, a speaker must know words of the language, syntactic principles, and some rules for conducting a conversation. In the adopted terminology, the rules of conversation can be labelled "Rules of File Keeping". There is an important difference between the knowledge of the lexicon and syntax, on the one hand, and the knowledge of conversational rules, on the other. The former type of knowledge is *speaker-internal*, in the sense that speakers do not have to take into account other speakers' knowledge. Speakers use terms like 'a cat', 'democracy', 'London' to talk about their concepts of the corresponding terms. A conversation is, by and large, mutually understandable because, although each speaker talks about his or her individual concepts, these concepts are, in most cases, similar to those of other speakers. The same is true about the syntactic knowledge. Speakers know that 'Mary likes John' is a good English sentence while 'Mary John likes' is not because of their internalised knowledge of some syntactic constraints, which is independent of other speakers' knowledge of these constraints.

By contrast, knowledge of the rules of conversation is different in that its implementation relies on speakers' capacity to make inferences about other speakers' representations of the conversation. Although the rules themselves are speaker-internal, this knowledge can be better labelled "conversation-internal": it implicates the speaker's capacity to go beyond their own internal representations and take into account representations of other participants in the conversation. No such requirements exist for the implementation of the syntactic knowledge. The use of definite NPs discussed in this chapter, illustrates the point. A speaker can felicitously utter sentences in (44), only if he or she makes sure that other participants in the conversation can build the same bridge between the two file cards as he or she does.

(44) a. I went to a wedding. The bride was wearing a blue dress.
b. I read a book and wrote to the bus driver.
c. I want to discuss the paper with HER (pointing).

To utter (44a), the speaker must be sure that the listener also possesses the relevant cultural knowledge that informs him or her about the intrinsic relation between a wedding and a bride. To utter (44b), the speaker must be sure that the listener is also aware that the book under consideration was recommended to me by a local bus driver. And to utter (44c), the speaker must be sure that his or her pointing to some female individual can be seen by other speakers. In all of these cases, the speakers' individual knowledge is not sufficient. It is not sufficient for me to know that I know who I am talking about in (44c), or that I know who recommended the book in (44b). The relevant knowledge is *conversation-internal* in the sense that I have to make sure that other participants in the conversation share it with me.

Clearly, speakers cannot directly access other speakers' minds to check whether they share the relevant knowledge. The only possibility is to use our *inferential capacity* to infer whether other participants do, or do not have the relevant knowledge. In other words, speakers cannot felicitously use definite NPs in (44) without making certain inferences about other speakers' knowledge. Thus, the two types of knowledge involved reflect the well-known distinction between necessary and probabilistic knowledge, that is something that is necessarily true (I know that bachelors are not married), and something that is, probably, true, but does not have to be (I know, and I believe other speakers know, that books have authors, so I can say "I read a book and wrote to the author", although, in principle, it does not have to be true). As discussed above, the second type of knowledge is implicated when a speaker constructs a bridge between two file cards in his representation of the discourse. Thus, we can formulate the following constraint on bridging (see also Hawkins 1978):

> **(45)** When bridging two file cards, make sure that other participants in the conversation will be able to build the same bridge.

This constraint can be satisfied on the basis of some inferences that, in turn, can be based on our world knowledge if we can assume (or infer) that other participants share this knowledge with us. The relevant shared knowledge can be Encyclopaedic (there is one Sun, I can say "the Sun"), or local ("the city hall", etc.). This constraint can also be satisfied if a speaker introduces a new Visual Situation Card by pointing to something. In this case, the speaker can infer that the listener sees the pointing and interprets it in the same way: Introduce a new card corresponding to the situation the speaker is pointing to. That is why pointing is necessary in the case of the deictic use of a definite NP. Without pointing, the constraint on file change stated in (45) is not satisfied. Even if a speaker introduces a new Visual Situation Card into his or her personal file, he or she cannot infer that other speakers will do the same. This inference becomes possible if the speaker informs other speakers about the relevant change in his individual file. The speaker can make the following inference: "I changed my file by adding a new card. I informed other speakers about this change by my use of pointing. Other speakers saw my pointing. They know what it means. They change their files accordingly, that is they introduce a new file card. Therefore, (45) is satisfied and the deictic use is allowed". If there is no pointing, speakers can make the following inference: "I changed my file by adding a new card. I did not inform other speakers. I know that they cannot know what is happening in my mind. Thus, I know that they are not aware of any changes in my file. They won't be able to make corresponding changes in their files. (45) is not satisfied. I cannot use a deictic NP".[10,11]

To summarise, the difference between our syntactic and discourse-related knowledge is that only the latter implicates our capacity to make inferences. These inferences are required in order to satisfy the constraint on bridging presented in (45). If speakers are somehow unable to make appropriate inferences, we might expect them to demonstrate certain problems in trying to follow the constraint on bridging. By contrast, no problems are expected with respect to their syntactic knowledge because the inferential capacity is not implicated in this case. I return now to the analyses of errors that children and Broca's aphasics make in their comprehension of pronouns. I argue that these errors are a manifestation of a deficit of their processing capacity required for making inferences about other speakers' representation of the discourse.

CHAPTER III

ANOMALOUS INDEXATION

In this chapter, I return to the results of acquisition experiments, and experiments with Broca's aphasics. The deficit observed in these two populations, I suggest, is due to certain limitations on resources needed for making inferences required for the correct deictic use of a definite NP. This explanation, which is close in spirit to the one proposed by Chien and Wexler (1990) is based on the argument that there is a specific relation between reference and indexation, and that children's (and aphasics') problem is closely related to this relationship.

1. Principle A and Principle B Constructions

As mentioned in Chapter I, children and aphasics demonstrate almost perfect performance on sentences with reflexives. They correctly accept sentences of type (1) when, in the experimental story, Father Bear washes himself, and correctly reject them when Father Bear washes somebody else.

(1) Father Bear washed himself.

This good performance is predicted on the proposed account because, in this case, no discourse-related inferences are called for. In a typical experimental situation, a subject sees a picture, or a story with toys. There are two characters: Father Bear and somebody else, say, Clown. When the subject hears the story, he or she creates a file where these two characters are represented by two different cards with two different numbers. Suppose Father Bear is washing himself. The subject hears sentence (1) and is required to judge whether there is any grammatical representation he or she can assign to this sentence in such a way that it would be a true description of the situation. Now, in syntax, NP *Father Bear* has an index. Because of Principle A, the only grammatical representation of this sentence is the one where *himself* receives the same index as its antecedent. In this case, the two NPs are coindexed, which means that in the discourse they must be represented by the same file card. In other words, the file card corresponding to the NP *Father Bear* contains information that he washed somebody represented in discourse by the same file card. This state of the file corresponds to the situation where Father Bear washed himself, and subjects correctly accept sentence (1) as a true description of this situation.

Suppose now Father Bear washed Clown. A file corresponding to this situation should contain two cards, with a number and an entry for each of the two cards:

(2) #1: IS FATHER BEAR & WASHED #2
     #2: IS CLOWN & WAS WASHED BY #1

As mentioned above, when subjects hear sentence (1), the only grammatical representation they can assign to this sentence is the one where the reflexive is coindexed with *Father Bear*. This means that *Father Bear* and *himself* are represented in discourse by the same file card. Such a file, however, has to contain a card with the following entries:

#1: IS FATHER BEAR & WASHED HIMSELF
(or: WASHED #1)

Because there is no such card in the subjects' file, they reject (1) as a possible representation of this situation.

Notice that the correct assignment of indices and, therefore, correct interpretation of (1), depends only on the knowledge of the relevant syntactic constraint, namely Principle A, and on the knowledge of how indices are interpreted in discourse. No inferences about other speakers' representation of the discourse is necessary because the only possible way of indexation is forced by syntactic principles. And this is the case independently of whether the antecedent is a referring expression as in (1), or a quantifier *Every Bear* (as in 'Every Bear washed himself'). Children (and aphasics) know that the reflexive must be coindexed with its antecedent, which prohibits acceptance of any situation where the washer and the person washed are different individuals. This knowledge, again, is syntax-internal and does not require any inferences.

How are pronouns different? Why do children and aphasics make significantly more errors in sentences of type (4)?

(4) Father Bear washed him.

Suppose subjects see a situation where Father Bear is washing himself and is *not* washing the clown. This situation can be correctly described by the following file:

(5) #1: IS FATHER BEAR & WASHED HIMSELF
(or: WASHED #1)

#2: IS A CLOWN

Now, when subjects hear sentence (4), they assign two different indices (because of Principle B) to the two NPs in this sentence. This means that, in the corresponding file, NPs *Father Bear* and *him* are represented by two different cards because different syntactic indexation corresponds to the existence of two different file cards (different indices are instantiated by different file card numbers). NP *Father Bear* is represented by, say, card #1. What about the pronoun? Pronouns are definite NPs, and, normally, they do not introduce new cards. Thus, *him* can be represented in discourse by incorporating it into an existing card, the card that represents the clown. The resulting file in this case would look like this:

(6) #1: IS FATHER BEAR & WASHED #2
#2: IS CLOWN & WAS WASHED BY #1

This file, however, is different from the true file given in (5), and the sentence should be rejected (and is rejected by normal adults) as a possible description of the situation.

Recall, however, from the discussion in previous chapters that, in some cases, a definite NP can introduce a new file card with a new index. It happens when a newly introduced card can be bridged to an old one. A card representing NP *the bride* can be bridged to the card representing NP *a wedding*. A card representing NP *the President* can be bridged to the Country Card inside the Situation Card. And a card representing deictic *her* can be bridged to the Visual Situation Card created by pointing to some female individual in the visual scene. In all of these cases, the new card has a new number that corresponds to a new index of the represented NP. Why can't speakers introduce a new card for the pronoun in (4), thus rescuing the sentence from a Principle B violation?

In Chapter II, I suggested that a change in an individual file is allowed only if the speaker makes sure that other participants in the conversation can make corresponding changes. For example, an accommodation of a new card through bridging it to an existing one is allowed if all speakers can build the same bridge. The relevant information can be based on some world knowledge (e.g. books have authors), or by some extra-linguistic means, for example by pointing. In this case the bridge is constructed between the newly introduced visual situation card and the card representing the deictic NP. The speaker, however, has to infer that corresponding changes have been, or can be, made in other speakers' files. Given that speakers cannot directly access other peoples' minds, the only way to do that is by way of inferences. Pointing allows speakers to make such inferences. If a speaker introduces a new file card (which will function as the basis for the bridge) by pointing to some visual scene, he or she can infer that other speakers see this pointing and interpret it as a signal to also introduce a new card and build a bridge. If no pointing takes place, the speaker can infer that other participants in the conversation will not change their files because they have not been provided with the necessary information.

Thus, the pronoun in (4) cannot introduce a new file card because conditions for building a bridge are not met. The pronoun is a definite NP, but the card it introduces is not bridged to any other card in the discourse. In fact, it could only be bridged to the Visual Situation Card, if there were one. In other words, the pronoun could only be used deictically. However, pointing is required in this case. If there is no pointing, there is nothing for the pronoun to be bridged to, and it cannot be represented by a new file card with a new index.

To summarise, the pronoun in (4) cannot have the same index because of Principle B, and if it has a different index, it can only be the index of the card representing the clown. Any other index would require bridging, which is not possible here because of the constraints on bridging.

Notice that, unlike sentence (1) with a reflexive, the correct assignment of indices in (4) requires more than knowledge of syntactic principles (Principle B, in this case). It also requires that the speaker be aware of, and be able to implement, the constraint on bridging. This knowledge and ability are crucially dependent on the ability to make inferences about other speakers' representation of the discourse. I suggest that the problem that children and aphasics demonstrate with these sentences is directly related to this requirement. Specifically, I suggest that a limitation on processing resources that these two populations exhibit may result in their incorrect introduction of new file cards. Here is what happens.

When children or aphasics see a situation where Father Bear is washing himself, but is not washing the clown, they create a file no different from that of normal adults. This file is shown in (5), repeated below.

(5) #1: IS FATHER BEAR & WASHED HIMSELF

    (or: WASHED #1)
    #2: IS A CLOWN

Like normal adults, when these subjects hear sentence (4), they assign it a representation where the pronoun and the subject have different indices. This is so because, as I argued, these people know Principle B. Thus, NPs *Father Bear* and *him* are represented in the discourse by two different file cards. Clearly, subjects can incorporate the pronoun into card #2. This, however, will result in a file that looks like (6), which is different from the true file (5). Subjects, thus, should reject the sentence.

Recall, however, that the idea behind these experiments is to see whether there is *any* grammatical representation that would allow subjects to accept the sentence as a correct description of the situation. For normal adults, it is impossible because there is no legitimate way to introduce a new card for the pronoun and avoid a Principle B violation.

Suppose now that, although subjects know all relevant rules and principles of syntax and discourse, their capacity to make inferences with respect to other speakers' representations is limited (some psycholinguistic evidence supporting this claim will be presented shortly.) In this case, speakers will have difficulties evaluating whether the constraint on bridging is satisfied because, as discussed above, this evaluation crucially relies on the ability to make inferences. In particular, speakers have to make inferences about other participants' representations of the discourse. For example, a normal adult speaker can infer that if he or she introduces the Visual Situation Card into the file to bridge it with another card, but does not point to anything, other speakers will be unable to build corresponding bridges in their files. Thus, normal adult speakers will not use a definite NP deictically without pointing[12].

I suggest that children and aphasics fail to make appropriate inferences about other speakers' representations of discourse and allow the deictic use of definite NPs without pointing. When they hear sentences of type (4), they attempt to find a representation that would be both grammatical, and true of the situation (as mentioned above, the idea behind all these experiments is to see whether there is any grammatical representation that would allow subjects to accept the sentence as a correct description of the situation. See Crain and McKee (1985) and Crain (1992) for more discussion). This can be achieved if they introduce the Visual Situation Card and bridge it with the card representing the pronoun. Now that they have made these changes in their individual files, they have to make sure that the constraint on bridging is satisfied. They have to compute whether other participants in the conversation are able to build corresponding bridges. And that is what they fail to do correctly. They fail to make correct inferences, and they may conclude that this constraint is satisfied. In this case, they accept the sentence because it does not violate any conditions, neither syntactic, nor discourse-related. They may also conclude that the constraints are not satisfied, and the new card cannot be introduced. In this case, they will reject the sentence because it violates the constraint on bridging. In other words, children and Broca's aphasics will sometimes accept these sentences, and sometimes reject them -- exactly as it was found in the relevant experiments.

2. Good Performance with Pronouns

In Section 1, I provided an explanation for the good performance on sentences with reflexives and poor performance on sentences with pronouns. There are, however, constructions where children and aphasics demonstrate significantly better performance with pronouns as well. First, recall Grimshaw and Rosen's experiment where they compared children's performance on grammatical and ungrammatical sentences. Children were presented with the same type of sentences (repeated below as (7)).

(7) Father Bear washed him.

When in the story Father Bear washed the clown (the second character), children correctly accepted the sentence 83% of the time, significantly more often than when Father Bear washed himself. The correct conclusion that Grimshaw and Rosen drew was that children do know Principle B of the binding theory. Although I agree with this conclusion, I disagree with their claim that children do not differ at all from normal adults in any relevant respect. As discussed above, in my account, children (and aphasics) are different in that their processing capacity is limited.

How does the proposed theory account for the difference between the grammatical and ungrammatical version of (7)? The explanation is, actually, straightforward. When the child (or an aphasic person) sees the situation where Father Bear washes the clown, he or she creates the file given in (8).

(8) #1: IS FATHER BEAR & WASHED #2
#2: IS CLOWN & WAS WASHED BY #1

When the child hears (7), he or she assigns the pronoun and the subject two different indices, as this is the only option allowed by the grammar. This corresponds to a file where *Father Bear* and *him* are represented by two different file cards. As a definite NP, the pronoun does not normally introduce a new card. It cannot be incorporated into card 1, however, because different indices are instantiated by different card numbers. But it can incorporate into card #2; in other words, its index can be instantiated with the number of card 2. This will result in exactly the same file as shown in (8), which is a true file of the experimental situation. Children, therefore, will accept the sentence as a grammatical and true description of the situation. Crucially, no inferences are necessary in this case to come up with such a representation. The deficit concerning processing capacity proposed in the previous section is simply irrelevant. Thus, the relevant difference between the grammatical and ungrammatical conditions is that the inferential resources are called for only in the ungrammatical case.

Individual subject analyses support this approach. In the ungrammatical case, some children, probably, are able to carry out the necessary inferential computations, and, therefore, will reject the sentence. Some children will (at least sometimes) fail to make the relevant computations and, therefore, will sometimes accept and sometimes reject the sentence. Other children in this case may decide to always accept the sentence. Various non-linguistic factors (including the child's general preference for saying Yes or No) may come into play when the child is unable to complete the necessary computations. The overall result, therefore, is around 50%. But in the grammatical case, all children will always accept the sentence (because no inferential capacity is implicated here, only syntax, which is something which does not differ from child to child). Therefore, the overall result is significantly better.

Children's and aphasics' performance on sentences with quantified antecedents is also significantly better than on sentences with R-expression antecedents. Thus, subjects correctly reject (9).

(9) Every bear washed him.

This improvement is also predicted. Recall that children's and aphasics' performance on sentences of type (4) was explained by their incorrect deictic use of the pronoun. The interpretation of the sentence was something like "Father Bear washed the individual I am looking at". In (9), however, such an interpretation is not possible. NP *every bear* is a quantificational construction, and it does not denote any specific individual to be pointed at. Thus, the deictic use is impossible in principle. Assuming that children and aphasics know the meaning of *every bear*, we can explain why their performance is correct. The pronoun cannot be coindexed with the subject because of Principle B. But its index has to be instantiated, that is, the NP has to be represented in discourse by some file card. In the absence of the possibility of deixis, this is only possible if the pronoun is incorporated into an existing card. Given that *every bear*, as a quantifier, does not introduce any card (see discussion in Chapter 3), the only possibility is to incorporate it into the card representing some other character in the story, for example the clown. This corresponds to a situation where every bear is washing the clown, which is not true of the story (only one of them washed the clown, and each of them washed himself.) Subjects, therefore, correctly reject the sentence, which, although grammatical, does not correctly describe the situation. Once again, no inferential capacity is required in this case because the deictic use is not an option.[13]

To recapitulate, a correct interpretation of sentences with R-expression antecedents requires both knowledge of Principle B, and the ability to make inferences about other speakers' representations of the discourse. Sentences with quantified antecedents, by contrast, only require knowledge of Principle B. Thus, these two types of sentences constitute a minimal pair. The difference in subjects' performance can, therefore, be interpreted as evidence for their knowledge of Principle B: a conclusion first drawn on the basis of this evidence in Chien and Wexler 1990.

Finally, a brief note on production versus comprehension. It has been noticed that the errors children make on sentences of type (7) are observed much more often in comprehension experiments than in natural production. Children never (or, almost never) produce these sentences. A more detailed discussion of the difference between production and comprehension patterns can be found in Bloom et al (1994).[14]

Such a discrepancy is not surprising, of course. To be precise, it would be surprising for an account that argues that children do not know Principle B, an account that, as far as I am aware, does not exist in the literature. I have argued that children's errors in comprehension is a result of their attempt to find a grammatical and true representation of the sentence, for example by interpreting the pronoun deictically. The deictic use, in turn, requires accommodation of a new card by bridging it to another, newly established card. As I suggested in Chapter II, bridging requires additional resources. It is quite natural, therefore, that children will attempt to use such a mechanism only if there is no other, less expensive way. In comprehension experiments, this is the only way to derive a grammatical representation that would give them a true description of the situation. In production, however, there is a much less expensive way. If the child wants to describe a situation where Father Bear is washing himself, there is no reason why she should avoid the easiest way of describing such a scene by saying that Father Bear washed himself (using the reflexive). Notice that in this case nothing beyond syntactic knowledge has to be used (Principle A), that is, the child does not have to use any discourse-related rules and make inferences about other speakers. The child does not need to introduce a new file card and bridge it to another one. The relevant syntactic knowledge is automatic and cost-free, and, everything else being equal, the child takes the easiest grammatical route. Children, therefore, correctly and fluently produce sentences with reflexives. A similar pattern also (*modulo* general difficulties with lexical access) exists for aphasic speakers.

3. Weak Pronouns

As suggested in the previous section, children make errors in those cases where pronouns are interpreted deictically, that is as referentially independent elements. It is interesting, therefore, to look at those pronouns that can only be interpreted as dependent elements. These are the so-called 'weak' pronouns . They are labelled so precisely because they can never be interpreted independently, or deictically. They can never be stressed, and in some cases they require phonological support. A typical example is Romance clitics and the English pronoun *it*. In English, for instance, strong pronouns (*him, her*) can be used deictically (as in (10)), but *it* cannot, as in (11):

(10) Pointing: I like him, her, and her.
(11) Pointing: *I like it, it and it.

Similarly, Italian clitics cannot be used deictically, as (c) demonstrates:

(12) Pointing: *l'amo
                 him like
                 I like him'

Another English example is clitic *'em*. This element is similar to Italian clitic pronouns in that it is necessarily referentially dependent. One can say:

(13) As for Bill, I really like'em.

Suppose now A asks B: "Who do you like?". B can point to C and respond with (14), but not with (15):

(14)   I like him.

(15)   *I like'em.

Thus, these elements cannot be used deictically. In terms of file change semantics, we can say that the weak pronouns can never be represented in discourse by an independent file card and receive their own index. They do not introduce a new file card and can be interpreted only through incorporation. In other words, they are necessarily coindexed with their antecedent (which does not have to appear in the same sentence, see Higginbotham 1985).

Regarding the acquisition of these elements, we predict that children should not make errors with weak pronouns of the kind they make with strong pronouns. Indeed, on the proposed account, errors occur as a result of the deictic use of a pronoun and introduction of a new file card. When this is not an option at all, as in the case of weak pronouns, no errors should be expected. Analyses along these lines were also presented in Avrutin and Wexler (1992).

There is evidence that this prediction is true. McKee (1992) reports results of an acquisition experiment with Italian-speaking children. Children were presented with sentences of type (16).

(16) Il Cavallo lo spoglia
'the horse him undresses'

In contrast to English-speaking children (who McKee tested in a parallel experiment), Italian children demonstrated almost an adult pattern of responses. That is, in cases where the horse undresses himself, children rejected (16) as a description of this situation. In other words, they overwhelmingly rejected the interpretation of *lo* as *Il Cavallo*. Rozalind Thornton (personal communication, February 1994,) in a pilot experiment, presented English-speaking children with sentences of type (17).

(17) The robot lassoed it.

In the situation, Robot tried to lasso some inanimate object but ended up with the lasso by itself. Thornton tested exactly those children who (in a different experiment) allowed the pronoun to refer to the subject in sentences of type (18):

(18) The Indian Man lassoed him.

Although the number of children was small, and it was just a pilot experiment, the results are suggestive. The same children who accepted (18) rejected (17)[15].

In summary, these results support the approach proposed in this book. Only in those cases where children attempt to interpret pronouns independently, do they make errors. When this is not an option, as in the case of weak pronouns, children's performance is significantly better.

An indirect result of these studies is that children at this age can use the syntactic information to distinguish weak and strong pronouns. It is not a trivial question how to figure out which pronominals are weak, and which are strong. Indeed, the fact that clitics appear in discourse only with a possible antecedent somewhere around does not tell the learner that it must be the case. In other words, the learner does not know from this positive input that an alternative would be wrong. A possible way of distinguishing the two types of pronouns is the realisation of differences in their X-bar properties (weak and strong pronouns may differ in whether they are heads or maximal projections, see Cardinaletti and Starke 1993). Although I do not discuss this issue here, the presented results suggest that children at this age have already figured out the relevant differences and can use them to distinguish between dependent and independent interpretations.

4. Principle C Constructions

Crain and McKee (1985) report that children correctly reject sentences of type (19). Similar results are reported by McDaniel, Cairns and Hsu (1990), Lust, Eisele and Mazuka (1992).[16]

(19) He washed Father Bear.

How can we explain the difference between children's performance on Principle B and Principle C constructions? Consider again (19). Let us apply to this sentence the mechanism of index assignment and interpretation discussed in previous chapters. When a speaker hears (19), he or she assigns it a syntactic representation. *He*, as an NP, must have an index. Suppose there are two characters in the story: Father Bear and Clown, both of whom have already been mentioned in discourse and are represented by two file cards (1 and 2).[17] The pronoun has an index i and gets incorporated into one of these cards (depending on how the listener interprets it). Suppose it is #1 (Father Bear). When NP *Father Bear* is encountered, it also bears an index, however, this index cannot be i because of Principle C. Thus, this NP can only receive a different index, for example j. This means that *he* and *Father Bear* must be represented by different file cards. In the absence of any specific contextual conditions (discussed in Chapter II), such a file corresponds to a situation where there are two different Father Bears, and one of them washed the other.[18] This, of course, is not the experimental situation simply because there is only one Father Bear in the story, and he does not wash anybody else except himself. Children, therefore, correctly reject this sentence. And, similarly to previous examples, if they interpret the pronoun as corresponding to another character in the story, for example Clown, they also reject the sentence because the obtained file represents a situation where Clown washes Father Bear, which is not the case here.[19]

The difference between Principle B and Principle C conditions, therefore, lies in what has to introduce a new card to avoid coindexation with the antecedent (see also Thornton and Wexler (in press) for a similar proposal). In Principle C experiments, it is an R-expression, and in Principle B experiments, it is a pronoun. If an R-expressions introduces a new card, it is necessarily interpreted as representing a new guise, which means, in the absence of some specific discourse conditions, a new individual. If a pronoun introduces a new file card, it may end up representing the same individual -- provided the speaker introduces a corresponding Visual Situation Card by pointing to some visual scene.

A natural question in this regard is why children cannot use the pronoun *he* in (19) deictically (that is, to bridge it to the visual situation card), assign it some index, and then give *Father Bear* a different index (the index of NP *Father Bear* introduced in the preceding discourse.)

This should be a possibility given that they interpret pronouns deictically in the Principle B studies. Recall, however, that in Principle B studies children are *forced* to attempt to use bridging as it is the only possibility for rescuing the sentence from ungrammaticality. The claim here is not that children want to "test" if deixis is the right thing to do any time they hear a pronoun. The claim is that when they try to find a *grammatical* representation of a sentence, they may resolve to deixis. In the case of Principle C constructions, there is no need for children to attempt the deictic use of the subject pronoun: The pronoun is fully interpretable as referring to an individual mentioned in the preceding discourse.

Clearly, if the coindexation of *he* and *Father Bear* is allowed in syntax (as in backward anaphora cases), children will allow coreference of these two NPs as well. For example, Crain and McKee (1985) report that children allow *he* to be *Grover* in about 75% of the time in sentences of type (20).

(20) After he jumped over fence, Grover drank some water.

He and *Grover* can be assigned the same index. Thus, when these indices are instantiated, these two NPs will be represented by the same file card. Children, therefore, are predicted to allow *he* and *Grover* to be the same person, which agrees with the reported results. 25% of the time, however, children chose another, extra-sentential antecedent (which was also correct). Children's tendency to accept a sentence if there is some grammatical representation for this sentence explains the 75% of acceptance reported by Crain and McKee.

CHAPTER IV

EXPERIMENTAL EVIDENCE FOR THE PROPOSED MODEL

1. Experimental Evidence for the Existence of two Different Mechanisms: Incorporation and Accommodation

As discussed in the previous chapter, there are two possible mechanisms of introducing a NP into discourse. The first, Incorporation, requires a minimum number of inferences, and can be expected to be very fast and automatic. NPs in this case are not represented by a new file card in discourse, and they do not receive a new index. The second mechanism, Accommodation, requires a certain amount of inferences (to build a bridge between two file cards), which may be expected to take more time. There are several experimental studies that bear on this issue. Here, I discuss an experiment reported by Acker and Boland (1992); for more references the reader is referred to their original work.

In a priming experiment, subjects were presented with sentences of type (1), which appeared on a computer screen. In half of the trials the recognition probe (*famous*) appeared in position marked as *1, and in half the trials it appeared in the *2 position. Subjects were to push a YES button if they thought the probe is a familiar word (that is, if it had appeared on the screen before). Moreover, in half of each of these conditions the subject of the second clause was a pronoun *she*, and in half it was a nominal anaphor *the star*. The response time was measured in each trial.

(1) The famous actress was interviewed by the white anchorman, but (she/the star)*1 was not cooperative*2.

The idea behind this design, which is relevant for the current discussion, is to see whether it takes subjects less time to establish reference for a pronominal than for a nominal anaphor, and whether this difference disappears at the end of the sentence. Presumably, the recognition of the probe will be faster when the referent NP (*the famous actress*) is accessed faster.

Acker and Boland's results are summarised in Table 1 and are presented for convenience as a graph in Figure 1.

	Position 1 (msec)	Position 2 (msec)
Nominals	730	706
Pronouns	703	718

Table 1: Mean Response Time

The difference between pronouns and nominals in Position 1 was statistically significant. The difference was also statistically significant between pronouns in Position 1 and Position 2, and between nominal in Position 1 and Position 2. The difference between pronouns and nominal was not statistically significant, although it was in the direction of significance. How can we interpret these results in terms of introduction of file cards? Consider first Position 1. Pronoun *she* does not introduce a new card. It is represented in discourse by incorporating into a previously existing card, namely the card representing *the famous actress*. *The star*, on the other hand, is not incorporated because (as in the case of *wedding: bride* discussed above) incorporation leads to identity, which is not the case here. Thus, it can only be accommodated by introducing a new file card and bridging it to the card representing *the famous actress*. This process is computationally more complex, which accounts for the difference between pronouns and nominal in Position 1.

Figure 1

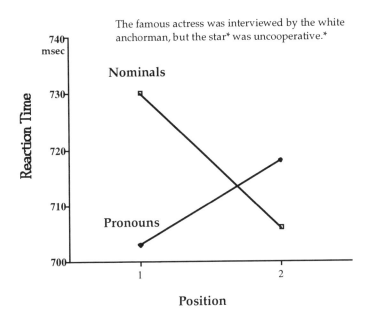

Consider now Position 2. Since pronouns do not introduce new cards, the recognition of the probe now takes longer simply because the distance to the referent has increased. For nominals, however, the situation is reversed. The relevant file card for NP *the star* has already been introduced, and the bridge has been established. Thus, the process of reaching the antecedent is no longer impeded by the necessity to bridge two cards, and subjects take approximately the same amount of time to access the referent as they take for pronouns.[20]

To summarise, the results discussed in this section show that the proposed difference between computational complexity of Incorporation and Accommodation finds empirical support from the real-time processing of pronominal and nominal anaphors.

2. Deictic Use of Definite NPs in Children's Discourse

So far we have considered certain cases where I argued that children interpret pronouns deictically. But what happens in production? Are children different in any way from adults in their use of definite NPs, pronouns in particular, in discourse? In this section I present several studies that show that children's use of definite NPs is different from adults'. In particular, children appear to allow the deictic use of definite NPs (both R-expressions, and pronouns) in cases where such a use by adults is unacceptable.

2.1 Pronominalization in Children's Discourse

Karmiloff-Smith (1981) reports the results of the following experiment with English- and French-speaking children. Three hundred and fifty children between the ages of 4 and 9 were shown a bound book containing six pictures. They were asked to tell what is happening in this book. The pictures in the book were as follows:

1. A little boy is walking along the road.
2. The boy sees a balloon-man.
3. The balloon-man gives the boy a green balloon.
4. The boy walks off with the balloon.
5. The balloon flies off into the sky.
6. The boy starts to cry.

Karmiloff-Smith reports that there is a change around the age of 6 in the way the children use pronouns. Here is a typical story told by English and French kids (age 4-6). *B* here stands for the boy, *M* for the balloon-man, and *GB* for the Green Balloon.

"He's (B) walking along ... and he (B) sees a balloon-man... and he (M) gives him (B) a green one... and he (B) walks off home... and it (GB) flies away into the sky. So he (B) cries."

French-speaking children:

"La il(B) se promene. La il(B) voit un bonhomme avec des ballons. La il (M) lui donne un ballonn.. un vert. La il (B) part chez lui ou a l'ecole. La il (GB) s'envole loin, tres loin. Ben, la il(B) pleure."[21]

As Karmiloff-Smith puts it, children "...treat each utterance as a separate unit and do not attempt to make any intralinguistic cohesion across pronouns in the different utterances" (p. 241). Interestingly, this pattern of pronominalization occurs at the same age as when children make errors in sentences like *Cinderella is pointing to her* (that is, when they allow *her* to be *Cinderella*). But this is exactly what is predicted if the incorrect interpretation of *her* in such sentences is due to its deictic use. It is important, however, to distinguish these results from the production studies. As mentioned in previous chapters, children do not make "Principle B errors" in their speech (that is, they do not say 'John washed him' meaning that John washed himself.) Why is it that they still use the pronouns incorrectly in the Karmiloff-Smith study? The answer is actually quite straightforward. In the context where John is washing himself, the most economical way to describe this situation also happens to be grammatical, that is to say 'John washed himself.' The use of a reflexive does not require the introduction of a new file card, and the relevant syntactic constraints are satisfied as well. As discussed above, there is no reason for children to use a pronoun. In comprehension, on the other hand, syntax imposes certain restrictions on the pronoun. These restrictions force children to find a solution at the level of discourse, which they, sometimes, fail to do. But in the Karmiloff-Smith study, syntactic constraints on the distribution of pronouns are irrelevant. Pronouns are the only anaphoric elements that can be used here. The correct use of pronouns still requires that the speaker make inferences about the listener, which results, in the case of children, in an abnormal pattern of pronominalization.

It is interesting that Cairns et al. (1994) reported the following findings. Children in their study insisted on the internal reference for the pronoun in sentences like 'The lion patted the tiger before he jumped over the fence.' Some children restricted their reference of 'he' to 'the lion', or to 'the tiger'; others allowed it to be either one. Most children did not allow the pronoun to receive its reference from outside the sentence. These findings are interesting because they demonstrate that children, when it is allowed by the grammar, prefer to use incorporation as a mechanism for establishing pronominal reference to bridging. Indeed, to interpret the pronoun deictically would mean that a new file card is introduced, and then bridged to the old 'visual situation card.' But a more economical mechanism of incorporation was possible in this study, a mechanism that did not require introduction of a new file card. Children, thus, opted for the more economical option of file keeping because nothing else forced them to do otherwise.

2.2 Children's Use of R-expressions

In the previous section we saw that children appear to use one type of definite NPs (pronouns) deictically even in those cases where adults do not allow this use. How do children use definite NPs that are R-expressions (names)?

It has been noticed by many researchers (e.g. Maratsos 1974, Warden 1976, De Villiers 1978, among others) that children sometimes use definite NPs without making sure that the other party in the conversation knows what they are talking about. The following two examples from the Childese database (McWinney and Snow 1985) illustrate the point.

(a) Sarah: The cat's dead.
Mother: What cat?
(b) Adam: Put it up, the man says.
Mother: Who's the man?

This (inappropriate) use of definite NPs has been also investigated experimentally. Warden 1976, for example, reports the following experiment. Children were presented with a story in cartoon form and had to tell the story to another child who could not see the pictures because of a screen. Each story involved four characters, for example:

> Picture 1: A dog is chasing a hen.
> Picture 2: A cow stops the dog, and the hen is hiding behind the cow.
> Picture 3: The hen has laid an egg.

Warden tested children aged three, five, seven and 9 years old, as well as a group of adults. The results are summarised in Table 2.

	First Mention (percent)	
	Definite NP	Indefinite NP
Adults	0	100
9 years	18	82
7 years	39	61
5 years	38	62
3 years	54	46

Table 2: Definite and Indefinite NPs (from Warden 1976)

As Table 2 shows, adults always used an indefinite article to introduce an NP for the first time. This was not the case for children. Children before the age of seven, allowed both definite and indefinite NP to introduce a new referent. Notice that this is (approximately) the same age when children make errors with the deictic use of pronouns both in Karmiloff-Smith's experiment, and in Principle B experiments. These

76   CHAPTER IV

data are consistent with the proposal that children allow the deictic use of NPs in those situations where adults don't.

Maratsos 1976 reports results of another experiment with four-year old children. The experimenter and the children played several games, one of which ('Down the Hill') is described below.

> "Down the Hill was played with a wooden hill, a car, and Fisher-Price toy boys and girls which fit conveniently into the cars. The child sat across from the experimenter at a round table. The hill, the car on top of the hill, and the toys were placed on the experimenter's side of the table out of the child's reach. The child was told that the experimenter would send the car down with a toy child in the car, and the child was to select a toy, one at a time, to be placed in the car. After the child had selected a toy doll for the car, it was rolled down the hill..." (Maratsos 1976, pp.80-81).

There were four conditions in this game. In one condition ('visible'), the child could see the toy boys and girls. In the second ('invisible'), there was a screen between the child and the toys so that the child could not see them. Moreover, in half of the 'visible' situations, and in half of the 'invisible' situations, there was only one boy and one girl ('singular'). In the other half of these conditions, there were several boys and several girls. The experimenter first named the toys (e.g. 'Here are a boy and a girl we can use'). Then, the child was asked: "Who shall we give a ride to now?". The number of definite and indefinite NPs used in each condition was recorded, and is summarised in Table 3.

Notice that in the 'singular' condition, children have some preference for definite NPs (which is also appropriate for adults) in both the 'visible', and the 'invisible' condition. The situation is different, however, in the 'plural' condition. In the 'visible' part of this condition, children correctly use an indefinite article to introduce a new referent only 54% of the time. In other words, in 46% of the time they use a definite NP without making sure that the listener knows what

EXPERIMENTAL EVIDENCE

	Accuracy (percent)	
	Singular	Plural
Visible	75% (*the*)	54% (*a*)
Invisible	77% (*the*)	89% (*a*)

Table 3: Percentage of Correct Use of Definite and Indefinite NPs

they are talking about. This deictic use of a definite NP becomes much less frequent in the 'invisible' condition. Presumably, the invisibility of the referent inhibits the child's use of deixis, which is quite understandable. Deixis means pointing, but if the objects are not visible, the only way to use deixis is by some sort of 'mental pointing', which may be argued to be more complex.

Notice also that children at this age (in both experiments) do not *always* use a definite NP to introduce a new referent, rather they allow either (correct) indefinite articles, or (incorrect) definite articles. These data do not seem consistent with a strong 'egocentricity' hypothesis that claims that children use NPs deictically because they do not care about what other speakers know. If this were the case, one might expect children to always use a definite NP because children always know what they are talking about. In fact, in Maratsos' experiment, children have some preference for a definite NP in the singular condition, which is appropriate for adults, too. Still, in the plural visible condition, their response is simply chance; that is, their preference for the deictic use disappears when such a use requires making certain computations in order to figure out if it is legitimate. This, however, does not happen, which, I suggest, favours the "resource limitation" account. Children, as I suggested above, incorrectly use definite NPs deictically in some cases because they cannot compute whether this use is legitimate. Failure to carry out the necessary computations leads them to make assumptions regarding the appropriateness of the deictic use. Sometimes children assume that it is appropriate, sometime they assume that it is not, which results in their 40-60% use of definite NPs in an inappropriate situation.[22]

3. Limitations of Inferential Capacity

One of the mechanisms that normal adult speakers use to indicate the deictic use of a pronoun is emphatic stress. In (2a), for example, the unstressed pronoun is interpreted as *Bill*. This is, presumably, due to the speakers' tendency to interpret clauses in parallel: the pronoun is in the object position, so it is interpreted as referring to the object of the higher clause (Grober, Beardsly and Caramazza 1978). To signal to other participants in the conversation that a different interpretation of the pronoun is intended, the speaker may use stress, as in (2b).

(2) a. John hit Bill and then Sarah hit him.
    b. John hit Bill and then Sarah hit HIM.

To correctly interpret stress, listeners must be able to make relevant inferences about the speaker's representations, that is to infer that the speaker intended a non-parallel, deictic use of the pronoun.

It is, therefore, interesting that children have been shown to be "insensitive" to stress. Maratsos (1973) reports that 5-year-old children sometimes interpret the stressed pronoun in (2b) as referring to Bill, that is in the same way as in (2a). This is consistent with the account proposed in previous chapters. Due to their limitations on processing resources, children fail to make correct inferences with respect to other speakers' intentional use of contrastive stress. Notice, however, that if children were completely "insensitive" to contrastive stress, we might expect them to demonstrate a 100% incorrect performance. This is not what happened. The chance level of their responses is consistent with the idea that they attempt to implement certain knowledge they have but (arguably because of the limited resources) fail to do that.

Even more interestingly, Maxfield and McDaniel (1992) have shown that there is a statistically significant correlation between children's understanding of contrastive stress and interpretation of pronouns. These researchers demonstrate that children who are sensitive to contrastive stress in sentences of type (2b) are less likely to accept sentences of type 'Father Bear washed him' on the interpretation where Father Bear washes himself. This result suggests that one and the same deficit is responsible for children's errors in Principle B conditions and conditions with stressed pronouns, exactly as argued in my account of the observed errors.

In a recent study (Avrutin et al, submitted), we have demonstrated that agrammatic Broca's aphasics show a similar pattern of responses. Aphasic patients were presented with pairs of pictures, the first of which introduced three characters (e.g. Mary, John, Bill) and depicted some action, for example John chasing Bill. The second picture contained three pictures: Mary chasing John, Mary chasing Bill, and an irrelevant filler. Subjects were given the following sentences and were asked to identify the picture that corresponds to the sentence. In half of the trials the pronoun was unstressed, and in the other half it was stressed (as indicated by the capitalised letters):

(3) First, John chased Bill, and then Mary chased him/HIM.

The control group always correctly identified the antecedent for the pronoun, switching its reference depending on the stress. Broca's aphasics, however, overall made two kinds of errors. First, in the unstressed condition, they correctly identified the object (Bill) as the antecedent of the pronoun *him* only 60% of the time, which is not significantly different from chance. This suggests that they were unable to process the complex structure in (3) for the purposes of identifying the antecedent. Second, in the stressed condition, they switched reference (that is, chose the subject John as the antecedent) only 61% of the time. This suggests again that, similar to children, they failed to make inferences about the reference of the pronoun based on the information supplied by the contrastive stress. It is important, however, that aphasic patients were not totally insensitive to the stress.

The difference between the choice of the subject (John) as the antecedent for the pronoun in the stressed and unstressed conditions was statistically significant in the right direction (higher in the stressed condition.) This result shows that the patients were sensitive to the stress and, in fact, tried to implement their knowledge. The results are different from the normal controls because these patients lack the necessary resources to implement their knowledge and, therefore, make errors in their choice.

Additional evidence for this claim comes from a control experiment also included in the above study. In this experiment, stress was also crucial for the correct choice of a picture, but unlike the first experiment, the choice did not depend on the discourse-related operations such identifying the correct referent for the pronoun. Subjects were presented with three pictures, one of which was an irrelevant picture, the choice between the other two depended on the ability to interpret stress, for example a picture of a black board and a picture of a blackboard (i.e. the choice between a compound noun and an adjective - noun pair.) The normal control group again correctly chose one of the two relevant pictures depending on the stress pattern given by the experimenter (in half of the trials the stress was on BLACK, and in the other BOARD was also stressed.) Unlike the first experiment, Broca's aphasics were almost perfect in this task: depending on the stress, they correctly chose either a black board, or a blackboard. The comparison of the two experiments once again suggests that the deficit exhibited by these patients is better characterised in terms of the syntax - discourse interface, in the sense that the discourse - related operations, such as establishing reference for a pronoun, require additional processing resource. Subjects with limited resources thus demonstrate a significantly worse performance than normal controls and than the same subjects on the tasks that do not involve the discourse - related operations.

The inferential capacity is implicated not only in the interpretation of deictic pronouns. In cases where there is more than one potential antecedent for a pronoun, speakers have to make inferences about its appropriate interpretation based, for example, on the meaning of preceding sentences. For instance, in (4a), speakers can infer that if somebody finds someone's pencil, it is this person who gives it to the other one. By contrast, if somebody wants someone's pencil, it is the second person who gives it to the first one. Thus, the interpretation of pronouns in (4b) is different from that in (4a).

(4) a. Jane found Susan's pencil. She gave it to her.
b. Jane wanted Susan's pencil. She gave it to her.

Wykes (1981), however, reports that children around the age of 5 make significantly more errors in acting out (4b) than (4a). Similar to the contrastive stress experiment, children fail to make relevant inferences: they (sometimes) interpret *she* in (4b) as referring to *Jane*. In another experiment, Wyke asked children to act out sentences of type (5).

(5) Jane found Susan's pencil. The pencil was red. She gave it to her.

In half of the trials, there was one pencil, one car and one book (which made the second sentence --"the filler" -- irrelevant: it supplied no information relevant for the interpretation). In the other half of the trials, there were three different pencils: red, yellow, blue (which made the filler relevant: it carried certain information that had to be taken into account). Children were shown to make significantly more errors in interpreting pronouns in the "relevant filler" condition than in the "irrelevant filler". Wyke argues that the increase in the amount of computations that children have to carry out overloads their inferential capacity, which results in an incorrect assignment of reference to the pronouns. And, consistent with my claim, children, unlike normal adults, make errors in these conditions precisely because their inferential capacity is limited. Converging results regarding children's inferential capacity are reported in Paris and Lindauer 1976 who argue that, around the age of 7, there is a change in children's ability to use inference for sentence recall.

Another experiment that is relevant for the current discussion was carried out both with children, and Broca's aphasics. These experiments were based on Swinney's (1979) priming experiment.

Swinney showed that, in normal adult speakers, both meanings of an ambiguous word are accessed. Thus, independently of the context speakers showed priming for both ANT and SPY in (6) when these probes were presented after the ambiguous word BUG.

(6) The FBI agent/The Landlord found bugs [PROBE] in the corner of the room.

Swinney, Nicol and Zurif (1989) and Swinney and Prather (1989) showed that Broca's aphasics and children demonstrate a different pattern. Namely, these populations show priming only for the most frequent meaning of the word, in this case for ANT independently of the context. The explanation that these researchers offered was that the lexical access is slowed down (at least in aphasics), thus only the most frequent meaning of an ambiguous word is activated by the time the probe is presented.

I would like to reinterpret these findings somewhat. The presented analysis is based on the view that what is crucially involved in priming is activation of some semantic net. Let us suppose, however, that priming actually is a manifestation of the subjects' inferential mechanism at work. Thus, the word NURSE is activated faster than CHAIR if it is presented after DOCTOR because the chain of inferences from *Nurse* to *Doctor* is shorter (faster, easier) than from *Chair* to *Doctor*. Suppose now (as proposed in this thesis) that children's and aphasics' inferential capacity is less than that of normal adults. This deficit will manifest itself not only in making incorrect inferences (as in the case of pronouns), but also in a general slow down of the inferential process. This slow down will result in what appears to be "priming for the most frequent meaning only." In fact, subjects whose inferential capacity is limited will be fast to establish only the easiest, shortest inferential link, that is the link between the probe and the most frequent meaning of an ambiguous word.[23]

CHAPTER V

POSSESSIVE PRONOUNS AND REFLEXIVES IN RUSSIAN

In this chapter, I discuss the distribution of possessive pronouns and reflexives in Russian and present experimental results of a study with native Russian-speaking children. The experimental results are shown to support the account of children's errors discussed in previous chapters. I begin with the theoretical issue concerning Russian possessive pronouns and reflexives.

1. Overview of Russian Possessives

Unlike English, Russian has in its inventory both possessive pronouns and possessive reflexives. Only possessive reflexives, however, can be used to refer to the subject of the sentence:

(1)   a. Ivan$_i$ slomal ?*ego$_i$/svoj$_i$ velosiped.
         Ivan broke   his   REFL bike
      b. Ol'ga$_i$ pokazala Marii$_k$ eë?*$_i$/$_k$/svoju$_i$/*$_k$ komnatu.
         Olga showed   to-Maria her   REFL   room

Developing the theory originally proposed in Hestvik 1990, 1991, 1992, I argued elsewhere that referentially dependent elements (e.g. pronouns and reflexives coindexed with another NP) must move at LF to a functional category (for more discussion see Avrutin 1994). As a result of this movement, possessive pronouns in Russian become locally bound in violation of Principle B. Possessive reflexives, on the other hand, move to INFL where they are correctly bound by the subject (but not the object) of the sentence:

(2) a. *[IP Ivan$_i$ [IP t$_i$ [VP [V slomal] [DP Det-ego$_i$ [NP t$_i$ dom]]].
      Ivan   broke   his   house
   b. [IP Ivan$_i$ [IP t$_i$ Infl-svoj$_i$ [VP [V slomal] [DP [NP t$_i$ dom]]].
      Ivan   REFL   broke   house

The relevant difference between English and Russian is accounted for straightforwardly in the following way. Abney (1987) discusses the structure as in (3) for English possessives. Although he ultimately chooses a somewhat different analysis, let us assume that English possessives, indeed, have the following structure:

(3)   [DP he [D 's [NP [dog]]].

Thus, the relevant difference between the English and Russian possessives (shown in (4) is that in English the pronoun is already in a functional projection (in [Spec, DP]) while in Russian, at S-structure, it is in a lexical projection (in [Spec, NP]).

(4)   [DP [D [NP ego [sobaka]]].

There is independent evidence for the proposed difference in the structure of the possessive. The extraction of the possessor is impossible in English, while it is perfectly acceptable in Russian:

(5)   *Whose did he walk dog?
(6)   c*'ju   on vygulival sobaku?
      whose he walk-past dog
      'Whose dog did he walk?'

Given the structure in (3), the extraction in English is impossible because *he* and *'s* do not form a constituent, and therefore cannot be extracted. No such violation arises when the extraction is from [Spec, NP], as it is in Russian.

The requirement that coindexed pronouns must be in a functional projection, therefore, is already satisfied in English at S-structure.

Moreover, assuming that he is the subject of DP, DP is a Complete Functional Complex (see Chomsky 1986), and therefore a governing category. The pronoun is free in its governing category and Principle B is satisfied. English does not exhibit the anti-subject orientation of pronouns (unlike Russian (1b)):

(7)　John$_i$ showed Bill$_j$ [DP he$_i$/$_j$ [D 's [NP room]]].

This is, of course, expected if the pronoun does not move out of DP: as in (3), *he* is already inside a functional category. Therefore, it can be coindexed with either the subject, or the indirect object.

Thus, the difference in binding possibilities between Russian and English possessive pronouns follows from the difference in their structural properties. Russian possessive pronouns are base-generated in [Spec, NP], while English possessive pronouns are in [Spec, DP]. I turn now to the discussion of experimental results with a group of Russian-speaking children. One of the goals of this study was to investigate children's knowledge of the distribution of possessive pronouns and reflexives in Russian.

2. Experimental Results

In this section, I present results of an acquisition experiment with a group of Russian-speaking children. A full description and discussion of this experiment can be found in Avrutin and Wexler 1992. The goals of the experiment were two-fold. First, we intended to replicate previously obtained results in another language. One of the reasons why such a replication is important is that, unlike English, Russian pronouns and reflexives are morphologically dissimilar (for example: *ego* 'him', *sebja* 'himself'). Thus, we do not expect any confusion on children's part regarding the pronoun-reflexive distinction. Second, we intended to investigate children's knowledge of the distribution of possessive pronominals, something that cannot be tested in English.

Sixteen Russian speaking children participated in the study, all of them living in the Greater Boston area. The children ranged in age from 4 to 7 years. All acquired Russian as their first language, and all were born in Russia. Both parents of each child were monolingual native Russian speakers. The children had spent most of their time in a Russian-speaking environment. Several children did not know any English at all as they were tested shortly after their arrival in the US. Three adult native speakers of Russian were also interviewed.

Procedure. The Truth-Value Judgement task (Crain and McKee (1985)) was utilised. The experimenter told the child a short story (staged as an event with props) in which characters did some action either to themselves, or to other characters. As the experimenter mentioned each action, he acted out the action using props such as toys representing each character. In this way, it was made easy for the child to understand the story.

At the end of each story, a puppet (a frog) would say something he believed had happened in this story. Children were trained to feed the puppet a toy ice cream if it said something right (that is, what, indeed, happened in the story), and a shoe, if he said something wrong (that is, something which did not happen in the story). Children received no feedback during the experiment: The experimenter did not tell the child whether his/her choice of response was correct or incorrect in a given situation. The three adults were tested in a slightly different way. One of the adults was shown the situations and made judgements as the children did. Two instances of each of the 17 conditions were given. For the other two adults, we didn't use the puppets, but simply described the situation and obtained judgements, on two sentences for each condition.

The sessions and materials. There were five experimental sessions per child, plus training. Four stories were told per session (occasionally more, depending on the child's willingness to continue playing) for a total of 20 stories. After each story the puppet said several sentences (all regarding the story). One to three of these were experimental sentences, the others were fillers. Fillers were inserted to avoid systematic "Yes", or systematic "No" responses. For example, if a child gave two "Yes" responses in a row, a definitely incorrect filler was inserted to elicit a "No" response. Four Russian verbs were used in all conditions: 'lizat' (to lick), 'teret' (to scrub), 'razrisovyvat' (to paint, to draw over), 'dut' (to blow). (Care was taken to avoid those verbs which could be used with a reflexive affix -sja). Each session was audiotaped. Either 2 or 4 sentences were presented for each of the 17 conditions. There were a total of 50 sentences (not counting fillers). The stories were presented in the same order to all the children. A sentence testing a particular condition appeared in first, second, or third position after different stories. Moreover, parallel pronoun and reflexive sentences did not appear together after the same story. This was done to avoid causing the child to use a contrastive strategy. For example, sentences with pronouns (e.g. Father bear scrubbed him) did not appear after the same story as did sentences with reflexives (e.g. Father bear scrubbed himself).

The English translation of a sample experimental story is presented below. Pronouns are shown in brackets here because in Russian their use is optional. To avoid any hint to the child, no pronouns or reflexives were used in any of the stories.

Boys and Bears Story

One day these three boys and this Father Bear went to the river to swim. Father Bear went in the water and began scrubbing (his) legs, (his) arms, (his) back, he scrubbed all over.

And the boys also got in the water and also began scrubbing (their) legs, (their) arms, and (their) heads, because they were very dirty.

Then, Father Bear said: "Could somebody please help me scrub (my) head?"

But these two boys - this one and this one - said: "No way, bear! We're too busy! We have to go home soon, and we still have to scrub (our) heads!

But this boy said: " O.k, I'll help you a little bit, but not too much because I have to scrub (my) head, too".

So he helped Father Bear a little bit - scrub, scrub - and then he joined other boys again. They were scrubbing (their) heads, and he scrubbed (his) head, too.

And Father Bear was left alone. He said to the boy: "Thanks a lot, maybe next time I'll help you, but now I am too busy, I want to go home clean" - scrub, scrub.

Puppet: 1) I know who scrubbed his head: Every boy.
2) Father Bear scrubbed him.
3) Every boy scrubbed himself.

A more detailed discussion of the experimental situations, as well as a summary of all results can be found in Avrutin and Wexler 1992. The results regarding personal pronouns and reflexives in Russian (a replication of the English experiment) were already mentioned in Chapter I. To briefly recapitulate, children's performance on sentences with reflexives was almost perfect (over 90% correct acceptance, and over 90% correct rejection). This was so for both R-expression NP antecedent, for quantifier *kazdyj* and for quantifier *kto*. Here is a summary of the experimental results (Group data are summarised in Table 1; Individual subject data are given in Table 2).

Children's responses to sentences with pronouns, however, were much worse. As in previous studies, Russian speaking children allowed *ego* 'him' to be *Papa Medved'* 'Father Bear' 52% of the time:

(8) Papa Medved' poter ego.
Father Bear scrubbed him

When the antecedent for a pronoun is a quantifier *kto* 'who', the children's performance was significantly better (83% of the time).[24] The difference between these two conditions is statistically significant ($F(1,15)=18.7$, $p< .01$). These results are not surprising in the light of previous findings. Once again, children demonstrate a good performance on sentences with reflexives, which can be interpreted as a demonstration of their knowledge of Principle A.

POSSESSIVE PRONOUNS

#	Sentence Type	Adult Resp.	% Child accept
1	Father bear scrubbed him.	No	52
2	Father Bear scrubbed his head.	No	56
3	Father Bear scrubbed himself.(True)	Yes	94
4	Father Bear scrubbed himself.(False)	No	3
5	Father Bear scrubbed self's head. (True)	Yes	94
6	Father Bear scrubbed self's head. (False)	No	2
7	Every Bear scrubbed him.	No	41
8	Every bear scrubbed his head.	No	50
9	Every bear scrubbed himself. (True)	Yes	97
10	Every bear scrubbed himself. (False)	No	6
11	Every bear scrubbed self's head. (True)	Yes	92
12	Every bear scrubbed self's head. (False)	No	8
13	I know who scrubbed him. Every bear.	No	17
14	Father Bear him scrubbed.	No	34
15	I know who scrubbed himself. Every bear.(True)	Yes	95
16	I know who scrubbed himself. Every bear.(False)	No	3
17	I know who scrubbed his head. Every bear.	No	20

Table 1. Group Responses to Experimental conditions

In Principle B constructions, however, children allow the deictic use of the pronoun, which is necessary in order for the pronoun to receive an index different from its antecedent. The difference between an R-expression NP antecedent and a quantified NP antecedent case was discussed in Chapter 3. Thus, these results can be explained in the same way as results with English-speaking children. And, once again, the crucial difference between pronouns and reflexives is that the interpretation of reflexives requires only the speaker-internal, syntactic knowledge.

CHAPTER V

TABLE 2
Individual Responses to Experimental Conditions (+ YES; - NO)

#	Sentence Type \ Age:	Adults	1 4	2 4	3 4	4 5	5 5	6 5	7 5	8 6	9 6	10 6	11 6	12 6	13 6	14 7	15 7	16 7	% acceptance by children
1	Father bear scrubbed him	-	2+ 2-	4+	2+ 2-	2+ 2-	3+ 1-	2+ 2-	3+ 1-	1+ 3-	2+ 2-	2+ 2-	2+ 2-	3+ 1-	4-	2+ 2-	1+ 3-	2+ 2-	52
2	Father Bear scrubbed his head	-	2+ 2-	2+ 2-	3+ 1-	4+	4+	2+ 2-	3+ 1-	4-	3+ 1-	4-	2+ 2-	4+	4-	4+	3+ 1-	4-	56
3	Father Bear scrubbed himself (True)	+	1+ 1-	2+	2+	2+	2+	1+ 1-	1+ 1-	2+	2+	2+	2+	2+	2+	2+	1+ 1-	2+	94
4	Father Bear scrubbed himself (False)	-	2-	1+ 1-	2-	2-	2-	2-	1+ 1-	2-	2-	4-	2-	2-	2-	2-	2-	2-	3
5	Father Bear scrubbed self's head (True)	+	2+	2+	2+	1+ 1-	2+	2+	2+	2+	1+ 1-	2+	2+	2+	2+	1+ 1-	1+ 1-	2+	94
6	Father Bear scrubbed self's head (False)	-	2-	2-	2-	2-	2-	2-	2-	2-	2-	4-	2-	1+ 1-	2-	1+ 1-	2-	2-	2
7	Every Bear scrubbed him	-	4-	2+ 2-	3+ 1-	3+ 1-	4+	2+ 2-	2- 4+	4-	4-	4-	4+	4+	4-	4-	4-	4-	41
8	Every bear scrubbed his head	-	2+ 2-	4-	3+ 1-	4+	4+	2+ 2-	2+ 2-	1+ 3-	2+ 2-	2+ 2-	4+	4+	4-	2+ 2-	4-	4-	50
9	Every bear scrubbed himself (True)	+	2+	2-	2+	2+	2+	2+	2+	2+	2+	2+	2+	2+	2+	2+	2+	2+	97
10	Every bear scrubbed himself (False)	-	2-	2-	1+ 1-	2-	2-	1+ 1-	1+ 1-	2-	2-	4-	2-	2-	2-	1+ 1-	2-	1+ 1-	6
11	Every bear scrubbed self's head (True)	+	2+	2-	2+	1+ 1-	2+	2+	2+	2+	2+	1+ 1-	2+	2+	2+	1+ 1-	2+	2+	92
12	Every bear scrubbed self's head (False)	-	2-	2-	1+ 1-	2-	2-	1+ 1-	1+ 1-	2-	2-	2-	2-	1+ 1-	2-	1+ 1-	2-	2-	8
13	I know who scrubbed him. Every bear	-	4-	4-	1+ 3-	4+	2+ 2-	4-	2+ 2-	4-	4-	4-	4-	1+ 3-	4-	1+ 3-	2-	2-	17
14	Father Bear him scrubbed	-	4-	2+ 2-	3+ 1-	4+	1+ 3-	2+ 2-	1+ 3-	4-	4-	4-	3+ 1-	4+	1+ 3-	2+ 2-	1+ 3-	4-	34
15	I know who scrubbed himself. Every bear (True)	+	2+	2-	2+	2+	2+	2+	2+	2+	2+	2+	2+	2+	1+ 1-	2+	2+	2+	95
16	I know who scrubbed himself. Every bear (False)	-	2-		2-	2-	2-	1+ 1-	1+ 1-	2-	2-	2-	2-	2-	2-	2-	2-	2-	3
17	I know who scrubbed his head. Every bear.	-	4-	2-	1+ 3-	4+	4-	1+ 3-	1+ 3-	2+ 2-	2-	2+ 2-	4-	3+ 1-	4-	2-	2+ 2-	4-	20

Let us turn now to possessive reflexives. Recall that, at LF, a reflexive in Russian adjoins to INFL. Thus, the LF representation of (9) is given in (10).

(9) Papa Medved' potjor svoju spinu.
    Father Bear scrubbed self's back
(10) Papa Medved' INFL-svoju potjor [t spinu].
    Father Bear INFL-self's scrubbed [t back]

The only acceptable LF representation of this sentence is such that the subject and reflexive possessive are coindexed. This means that in discourse the two NPs are represented by the same file card and they must be interpreted as identical individuals. Thus, when in the story Father Bear scrubs his own back, the sentence is true, and if he scrubs someone else's back, the sentence is false. Children once again demonstrated knowledge of this condition. Overall, they correctly accepted the true situation 94% of the time, and they correctly rejected the false situation 97% of the time.

The situation with possessive pronouns was again different. Recall the analyses of these elements proposed at the beginning of this chapter. Consider sentence (11).

(11) Papa Medved' potjor ego spinu.
    Father Bear scrubbed his back

When a listener hears NP *Papa Medved'*, he or she assigns it an index. When pronoun *ego* is encountered, it must also receive an index. If the pronoun receives a different index, then, in discourse, it is represented by a different file card, which means that Father Bear scrubs someone else's back. Thus, children will not take this representation as being a true description of a situation where Father Bear is scrubbing his own back. But what happens if the pronoun receives the same index as the subject? Notice that the pronoun has moved to Det (or, it could move to another functional category, INFL, but this will not make any difference). In either case, however, the resulting representation violates Principle B, and the sentence is ruled out. This is what happens for adults, and that is why this sentence is unacceptable. The situation is somewhat different for children. As I argued for other cases of their errors with pronouns, children may try to rescue the sentence by using the pronoun deictically. This means, again, that it would receive a different index, and would be interpreted by bridging to the situation card. But, as I argued above, such a use requires that the constraint on bridging be observed. In attempting to compute these conditions, children get lost and may sometimes assume that this constraint is, in fact, satisfied. In this case, they will allow the possessive pronoun to be contraindexed with the subject, but to be "referring" (in an indirect sense) to the same entity. And, once again, if the antecedent is a quantifier *kto* 'who', the pronoun cannot be interpreted deictically (see discussion above), and children are predicted to show a better performance. The experimental results confirmed this prediction. In cases where the antecedent was an R-expression (e.g. Father Bear), children overall incorrectly accepted the sentence 56% of the time. When the antecedent was *kto* 'who', the performance was much better: only 20% of acceptance (the difference is statistically significant: $F(1,15)=16.4$, $p < .01$).

Another interesting result of this study (an indirect result of the condition with possessive pronoun and *kto* 'who' antecedent) is that children appear to know that pronouns in Russian move at LF to a functional category. If they did not know this constraint, the possessive pronoun would not have to move out of NP, and the sentence would be acceptable even under coindexation of the pronoun and subject. Thus, children's rejection of the sentence can be taken as (indirect) evidence of their knowledge of this condition.

CHAPTER VI

PLURAL PRONOUNS[25]

1. Distributivity and Binding in Child Grammar

In this chapter I look at children's understanding of the discourse representation of plural pronouns, and their understanding of the relationship between discourse and syntactic representations.

Plural pronouns are especially interesting in this respect. A plural NP can be interpreted either as denoting *a collection* of individuals ('collective reading'), or each of the individuals ('distributive reading'). The following example illustrates the point:

(1) John and Mary went to Paris last year.

Plural NP *John and Mary* can be interpreted either distributively, or collectively. Thus, (1) can either mean that John went to Paris in June, and Mary in July, or it can mean that they both together went to Paris some time last year. The question is how these two different readings are represented in syntax and discourse. It was proposed in the literature (and discussed in the next section) that the distributive reading is represented in syntax as a quantificational construction, while the collective reading does not have this property. In terms of file change semantics, it means that only under the collective reading is the plural NP represented in discourse by a file card, which will stand, in this case, for the group of individuals (with the group being a discourse referent by itself.) It follows then that only under collective reading a plural NP can be interpreted deictically. At the same time, I argued that children sometimes have problems with the correct use of deixis, while they have no problems with the syntactic distribution of pronominals. Thus, with respect to plural pronouns, we might expect that children will exhibit a different pattern of responses to collective and distributive situations. In fact, if it is the case, such a result would be evidence for a specific linguistic theory that argues that distributive and collective readings have different syntactic and representations. A population (children in this case) that has problems with a discourse representation but no problems with syntactic representation are predicted on the basis of this theory to show differences in two conditions. This hypothesis was put to the test in the following experiment conducted in collaboration with Rozalind Thornton (Avrutin and Thornton 1993.)

According to Heim, Lasnik and May (1991), differences between the collective and distributive interpretations of plural NPs are represented at LF. At LF, plural NPs interpreted distributively are accompanied by a distributive operator, and are quantificational. On the collective interpretation, plural NPs have no such operator, and are referential. Heim, Lasnik and May (HLM) propose that the difference in interpretation surfaces when plural NPs interact with principles of Binding Theory. Let us see now what predictions this theory (in conjunction with the approach adopted in this book) makes with respect to children's performance.

Recall first that some young children allow a pronoun to refer to a local antecedent in sentences like (2), in apparent violation of Principle B.

(2) Mama Bear is drying her.

By contrast, when the antecedent of the pronoun is a quantified NP, as in (3), these children are more like adults in rejecting an anaphoric relation between the antecedent, *every bear*, and the pronoun, *her*.

(3) Every bear is drying her.

I have argued that the difference in performance is due to the children's problem with deictic use of definite NPs. More specifically, I suggested that they allow this use in situations where normal adults don't. As discussed above, such a use results in a contraindexation of the pronoun and its antecedent, as in (4).

(4) Mama Bear$_i$ is drying her$_j$.

Quantified NPs, on the other hand, have no inherent reference (thus, no discourse considerations are involved), the only way to link *every bear* with *her* is by coindexation, with the pronoun being interpreted as a bound variable. Coindexation results in a violation of Principle B, however. Children's rejections of (3) can therefore be understood as demonstration of their knowledge of Principle B.

Children who have problems with the correct use of deixis provide an ideal test of Heim, Lasnik and May's (1991) theory of how plural NPs interact with Binding Theory. As previous experiments have demonstrated, these children are sensitive to the distinction between referential and quantificational antecedents. This is exactly what distinguishes the collective and the distributive readings of plural NPs on HLM's theory.

2. Plural Pronouns

Plural NPs can either denote a collection of individuals or they can quantify members of some collection. In quantificational contexts, where members of a group are treated separately, the plural NP is accompanied by a distributive operator (Link, 1983, 1987, Roberts, 1987, Heim, Lasnik and May, 1991). According to Heim, Lasnik and May (1991), the distinct interpretations of plural NPs are represented at LF. There, the Binding Principles apply to the indices assigned to plural NPs and to the distributive operator, D. Consider two of the interpretations that can be given to the plural NP *the Smurf and the clown* in (5).[26]

(5) The Smurf and the clown dried Big Bird.

In one interpretation, the plural NP could be used to refer to a group who, together, dry Big Bird, say with a large towel. This context will be called a 'collective context'. The representation for the collective context of (5) is shown in (6). Another interpretation of (4) corresponds to contexts in which the Smurf and the clown each dry Big Bird in different drying events. Such a context will be called a 'distributive context'. The representation in (7) corresponds to a distributive context for (5).

(6) [The Smurf and the clown]$_i$ dried Big Bird$_k$.

(7) [[The Smurf and the clown]$_i$] D$_j$] dried Big Bird$_k$.

In (8), *Big Bird* is replaced with the plural pronoun *them*: Principle B is now relevant to the representations.

(8) The Smurf and the clown dried them.

(9) *[The Smurf and the clown]$_i$ dried them$_j$.

(10) *[[The Smurf and the clown]$_i$] D$_j$] dried them$_j$.

Coindexation is ruled out in both (9) and (10) by Principle B. In (9), the relationship between the NPs denoting the two sets is one of coreference. The NP *the Smurf and the clown* shares the same index as the NP *them*. In (10), the operator D distributes over the set denoted by *the Smurf and the clown*, and this operator is coindexed with the plural pronoun *them*.

Recall now the interpretation of indices that was discussed in Chapter II. When the antecedent is a quantifier, as in (10), the coindexation is interpreted as representing a bound variable (syntactic) type of dependency. When the antecedent is a referring definite NP (as in (9)), the coindexation represents identity of file cards. *The Smurf and the clown* is a referring NP in (9) because, under collective reading, it denotes a set of individuals, which can be represented in discourse with a file card.[27] What is important is that the plural pronoun in this case is *not* a bound variable. Although children will not accept the representation in (9) because it violates Principle B, they may attempt to interpret the pronoun deictically, in the same way they do in (4). If they decide that the deictic use is allowed (the constraint on bridging is satisfied), they will accept the sentence in (8), which (for them) will have representation in (11).

(11) [The Smurf and the clown]$_i$ dried them$_j$.

Notice that such a case of 'coreference under contraindexation' is possible only for pronouns with referential antecedents, i.e. only in collective contexts. In distributive contexts, the relationship is one of bound variable anaphora, and this is ruled out by Principle B *already in syntax*. If this distinction between plural NPs interpreted collectively and distributively appears in children's responses to sentences like "The Smurf and the clown dried them", this would be compelling evidence of the psychological reality of the D operator and its proposed interaction with Binding Theory at LF. This possibility is investigated in the experiment that follows.

3. Experiment

Thirty-three children between the ages of 3;10 and 4;10 (mean age 4;4) participated in the study. All were native speakers of English, tested individually at daycare centers in Storrs, CT and Arlington, MA. Children were tested using the Truth-Value Judgement task developed by Crain and McKee (1985).

The test battery consisted of sentences like (8), presented in both collective and distributive contexts, with four trials of each type. Each story has four characters. In the story (8), for example, in addition to the Smurf and the clown, there are two characters who are potential referents for *them*. In the collective context, the Smurf and the clown refuse to dry these other two characters, and use a big towel to (collectively) dry themselves instead. Children who allow the deictic use of pronouns should take *them* to be the Smurf and the clown and therefore should say "Yes" in this context. Children with the adult grammar, however, should take *them* to refer to the other two characters, and should say "No" to (8).

The distributive context contains two separate events. In the first event, the Smurf won't dry the other characters, just himself. In the second event, the clown refuses to dry *them*, and dries himself instead. This context is assumed to give rise to a distributive interpretation of the plural NP. If so, taking *them* to refer to the Smurf and the clown would violate Principle B. That is, children should reject (8) in the distributive context because neither the Smurf nor the clown dry *them* (the other two characters). An example of a "collective" and "distributive" story is given below.

COLLECTIVE STORY:
"The baby (B) and the troll (T) dried them"

This is a story about swimming. Here is the pool and these guys are all going swimming. These two boys are big boys, so they go swimming in the deep end. The baby and the troll are small, so they go swimming at this end of the pool, where the water isn't very deep. They have a lot of fun -- splash splash splash splash <troll and baby splash>.

After a while, the baby and the troll get cold, so they get out.

B & T: "Oh, that was fun. Where's our towel," they say. "Oh, there it is".

And they get their big towel, and wrap it all around both of them and they can get dry <baby and troll dry with the shared towel>.

B & T: "That's better. Now we're warming up."

Then the big boys get out of the pool, and go over to the baby and troll.

Big boys: "We didn't bring anything to get dry with. Could you dry us?

B & T: "Sorry, we can't dry you. This towel is only big enough for the two of us, and we're still using it." <repeat twice>.

TARGET: The baby and the troll dried them

DISTRIBUTIVE STORY:
The Smurf (S) and the troll (T) dried them.

This is a story about a rainy day in the park. These two clowns were sitting on a park bench. It was raining, and all the kids were playing inside. So they were feeling a little bit sad.

Clowns: "I hope it stops raining soon. We're getting wet. Maybe someone will come by soon, and lend us a towel."

Just then a Smurf comes by, pulling his wagon.

Clowns: "Hey, Smurf. Do you have anything you could dry us with. We're getting a bit wet, and we forgot to bring a towel"

Smurf: "Well, I do have a towel on my wagon. But it's just a small one. I can't dry you. It's not big enough. It's only big enough for me to dry my hat and all my body. <Smurf dries himself>. Sorry, but I have to go now - my friends are waiting for me. <Smurf leaves the scene>.

Clowns: "Oh well, he wouldn't dry us. But maybe someone else will come by".

Just then, a troll came running up, holding his briefcase.

Clowns: "Excuse me, troll. Do you have a towel? We're getting wet, here. Could you please dry us?"

Troll: "Um, well I'm in a terrible rush, because I'm late for work. But I could check quickly in my briefcase <opens briefcase>. Oh yes, I do have a towel. But it's just a very small one. And it's not very fluffy. I'm sorry, guys. But I better use it just to dry my body. <Troll dries off>. Oh no, I'm very late. I have to go. I'm already ten minutes late. Bye. <Troll runs off>.

TARGET: The Smurf and the troll dried them.

The experiment also included control sentences like (12), to ensure that the children allowed both the collective and distributive interpretations of plural NPs (Crain and McKee, 1985, Lasnik and Crain, 1985). We reasoned that only children who could assign a distributive interpretation in the control condition in (12) would be able to distinguish collective and distributive interpretations in test sentences like (8). The control sentences were based on contexts devised by Miyamoto and Crain (1991). Consider a situation in which there are two turtles, each with two pet bugs. In the experiment, Kermit the Frog's description established that the plural pronoun *they* was being used collectively, as in (12a), or distributively, as in (12b).

(12) a. I know how many bugs they have. Four. (=collective)

b. I know how many bugs they have. Two. (=distributive)

For adults, both (12a) and (12b) are accurate descriptions of the situation: "Four" is an appropriate answer when the pronoun is interpreted collectively, and "Two" is appropriate for the distributive interpretation. Children who assign both interpretations should say "Yes" to either of Kermit's descriptions. Children who assign only a collective interpretation, however, would say "Yes" to "Four", but "No" to "Two". Children with only the distributive interpretation should show the opposite pattern of responses.[28] There were four controls; two tested the distributive interpretation, and two tested the collective interpretation.[29]

4. Results

The 33 children accepted sentences like (8) in collective contexts on 50% of the trials. Of the 33 children, 17 children responded as adults, rejecting every trial presented in the collective context. These children were not tested further.[30] The remaining sixteen children accepted the collective interpretation on at least three of the four experimental trials, and were designated as the target group for testing the same kinds of sentences in distributive contexts. The target group allowed coreference in collective contexts 93% of the time. In the distributive contexts, by contrast, they allowed the pronoun to refer to the plural NP significantly less often, only 42% of the time ($F(1,15 = 36.92)$, $p <$ .001). The results are stronger than the numbers suggest, however, once the findings from the control condition are taken into account. It turned out that four children consistently rejected the distributive interpretation of the control sentences, as in (12). These children accepted test sentences like (8) in both the collective and distributive contexts. Because these children only assign a collective interpretation to plural NPs, their responses to the test sentences have no bearing on the HLM account[31]. Based on these observations, these four children were excluded from a final analysis of the data, which focused on the 12 children who allowed the distributive interpretation of plural NPs in the control condition. The responses of this group of children were quite different in the collective and distributive contexts. They accepted test sentences in the collective context 93% of the time, but only 27% of the time in the distributive context $(F(1,11) = 98.79, p < .001)$.

5. Conclusions

The results show that most four-year-old children distinguish the collective and distributive interpretations of plural pronouns. The fact that the majority of children accepted a collective interpretation of sentences like (8), but rejected a distributive interpretation of such sentences, suggests that distributive contexts force a quantificational representation. This can be interpreted as further evidence of the distinction between quantification and reference. The results can be seen to support proposals such as that of HLM which advance a syntactic difference between distributive and collective readings of plural NPs.

These results also show that the difference between children's responses to sentences like "Every Bear washed him" and "Father Bear washed him" is not due to their problems with lexical quantifiers (as was suggested, for example, in Grimshaw and Rosen 1990). In both collective and distributive readings the plural antecedent has the same lexical form: *the Smurf and the clown*. Thus, the relevant difference is in the interpretation of the antecedent (whether it is a quantificational, or referential expression), more specifically whether only syntactic knowledge is implicated, or the ability to carry out necessary computations about other speakers' representations of the discourse. Consistently with the general approach proposed in this book, children's errors with collective pronouns can be due to their incorrect use of deixis. Crucially, because this interpretation involves relationship between file cards, errors are predicted to be with collective, not distributive (quantificational) plural pronouns. The results of this experiment demonstrate that it is, indeed, the case.

CHAPTER VII

CHILDREN'S INTERPRETATION OF THE DISCOURSE-DEPENDENT REFLEXIVES[32]

So far we have been concerned with the interpretation of pronouns and errors that children make in this interpretation. We have seen that this interpretation requires a coordination of specific syntactic constraints (e.g. Binding Principles) and constraints at the level of discourse. It has been proposed that children posses all required syntactic knowledge but may have problems with implementing their knowledge of the discourse-related constraints, specifically constraints on bridging.

Regarding reflexives, we have assumed so far that their interpretation requires access only to syntactic principles, specifically, Principle A of the Binding Theory. Free from discourse constraints, these elements are "purely syntactic" in nature and, as such, do not cause any problems for children.

This view, however, is not completely accurate. As discussed below, in certain cases reflexive elements do require access to discourse and their interpretation is subject to both syntactic and discourse-related principles. These reflexives are known as *logophors* (see, for example, Clements 1975, Sells 1987). Before turning to the discussion of logophors, it is important to note that these elements provide an interesting test for the view adopted in previous chapters. Indeed, if children's errors with pronouns are due to the problems at the discourse level, one can predict that children will have troubles with interpreting logophoric reflexives as well. At least, children should be expected to make more errors with reflexives that are logophoric (i.e. require access to discourse) than with "purely syntactic", non-logophoric reflexives (i.e. whose interpretation does not require access to the discourse). Such a comparison was the goal of the two experiments reported in this chapter.

Before turning to the theoretical basis for the experiment discussed in this chapter, it is important to clarify the goal of this project. As discussed in the introduction, psycholinguistic research is to address two kinds of questions: Where the deficit is located and, given this deficit, how we can explain the abnormal patterns in experimental situations. Crucially, the second question relies on the understanding of a particular system to which the deficit is attributed. In the absence of a well-formulated linguistic theory, explanations of children's (or aphasics') errors are bound to be vague. It does not mean, however, that answering the first question (regarding the location of the deficit) is, by itself, an uninteresting or an unimportant question. The location of the deficit, in fact, is the first step towards its better understanding. This, I believe, is the situation that characterises experimental projects on comprehension of logophors addressed in this chapter. To the best of my knowledge, the exact distribution of logophors is still somewhat a mystery. While there have been various attempts to come up with theories explaining how these elements receive their reference (see discussion below), they often remain vague. The goal of this chapter, therefore, is not to provide a new theory of logophoricity. Nor will I attempt to give a precise characteristic of how children interpret these elements. The goal of this chapter is limited to answering the first question. The results presented here will provide further evidence for the claim advanced in previous chapters, specifically, that children possess the relevant syntactic knowledge of the distribution of reflexives. Their problems stem from non-syntactic, discourse-related factors.

Let me first outline the theoretical approach adopted in this study. This approach is different from the one presented in previous chapters and is based, mainly, on the work by Reinhart and Reuland (1993).

1. The Standard Binding Theory (SBT), Reflexivity and Logophors

Chomsky's version of the Binding Theory, and of Principle A, in particular, as introduced in previous chapters, requires that a reflexive has a local c-commanding antecedent (the binding requirement). Many researchers, however, noticed that there are counterexamples to this requirement. For instance, the following sentences are grammatical, although the antecedent either does not c-command the reflexive, or is not local (from Reinhart and Reuland 1993, (2) is attributed to Zribi-Hertz, 1989):

(1) Max boasted that the Queen invited Lucie and himself for a drink.
(2) Bismarck's impulsiveness has, as so often, rebounded against himself.

The grammaticality of these (and similar) structures was one of the reasons for the reformulation, or, rather, an alternative approach to the Binding Theory. This reformulation was proposed by Reinhart and Reuland (1993) and is known as the Reflexivity theory.

Both the SBT, and the Reflexivity are theories about the syntactic constraints on establishing reference for certain linguistic elements. But while Chomsky's version of the Binding theory is based on the notions of the C-command, locality and co-indexation, the Reflexivity theory characterises the distribution of pronominal elements in terms of conditions on predicates. In this view, the chief function of the binding theory is to disallow co-arguments of a predicate to be coindexed unless the predicate is reflexive marked, because, as Reinhart and Reuland point out, "a universal property of natural language seems to be that reflexivity must be licensed" (p. 662). This reflexive marking is either specified intrinsically in the lexicon, or obtained by using a SELF-anaphor to lexically mark it. Thus, a simple set of conditions on reflexivity can give rise to the same distribution provided by the binding theory:

Definitions
a. A predicate is *reflexive* if and only if two of its arguments are coindexed.
b. A predicate is *reflexive-marked* if and only if it is lexically reflexive, or if one of its arguments is a SELF-anaphor.

Conditions
A: A [syntactically] reflexive-marked predicate is [semantically] reflexive.
B: A [semantically] reflexive predicate is [syntactically] reflexive-marked.

(Reinhart and Reuland 1993, p. 663).

To illustrate these principles, consider (3) and (4).

(3) Mary$_i$ likes herself$_i$
(4) *Mary$_i$ likes her$_i$

Predicate *like* in (3) is reflexive-marked because one of its arguments is a SELF-anaphor (*herself*). Thus, this predicate is required to be reflexive. This requirement is satisfied because the two arguments are co-indexed. In (4), on the other hand, the predicate is reflexive because the two arguments are co-indexed, but, contrary to Condition B, it is not reflexive-marked (none of the arguments is a SELF-anaphor, and the predicate is not intrinsically reflexive). When the predicate is intrinsically reflexive, as in Dutch (5), the sentence once again is grammatical because the reflexive predicate is reflexive-marked (SE stands for a Simplex Expression, which does not have the capacity to reflexivize the predicate.)

(5) Max wast zich   (Dutch)
    Max washes SE

Importantly, these conditions apply only to reflexives that are co-arguments with their antecedents. Condition A does not say anything about the distribution of pronominal elements which are not co-arguments with their antecedents. This usage, termed *logophoric use*, is illustrated in (6), (7), (8) and in (1), (2).

(6) Lucie$_j$ counted 5 tourists in the room apart from herself$_j$.
(7) Bismark$_j$'s impulsiveness has, as so often, rebounded against himself$_j$.
(8) A picture of myself$_j$ would look nice on this wall.

According to Reinhart and Reuland, these reflexives are not under the jurisdiction of Principles A and B. In their model, a distinction exists between the grammatical function of anaphors as reflexivizers and their logophoric use:

> "... the binding theory governs only the use of anaphors in reflexivization contexts. In these contexts, a SELF-anaphor which does not function as a reflexivizer is ruled out. But in all other contexts, condition A does not rule out an anaphor, which can then be used logophorically" (p. 672).

If the binding theory is not applicable to the logophoric use of anaphors, another, different set of conditions must govern their use. According to Reinhart and Reuland (1993), Sells (1987) and other researchers these conditions lie within the realm of discourse and pragmatics. Logophoric elements (that in a number of languages may have a different morphological form) may have a distribution distinct from that of other pronominals. Roughly, the antecedent of the logophoric element must be the one "whose speech, thoughts, feelings, or general state of consciousness are reported" (Clements 1975, 141). The concepts involved in the theory of logophors are qualitatively different from those involved in syntactic theory. Sells (1987), for example, providing evidence from various African languages (as well as from Japanese and Icelandic) describes the distribution of logophors in these languages in terms of the following primitive (discourse-related) concepts:

> SOURCE: one who is the intentional agent of the communication.
> SELF: one whose mental state or attitude the content of the proposition describes.

PIVOT ("point of view"): one with respect to whose (space-time) location the content of the proposition is evaluated.

Similar analyses were offered by Mailing 1986 and Anderson 1986 for Icelandic logophors, and by Hellan 1988 for Norwegian.

Although a precise characterisation of logophors is still an open question, one important property of these elements should be emphasised. Unlike syntactic reflexives whose distribution is subject only to syntactic constraints, the interpretation of logophors requires accessing the discourse level of representation. This is so because the notions of the SOURCE, SELF, PIVOT are characteristics of the discourse structure. Thus, establishing reference for a logophoric reflexive depends on the speakers' ability to access the discourse and to determine the relevant referents.

Let me illustrate the role of some of these notions by an Icelandic example from Mailing (1984) and a Japanese example from Sells (1987). The Icelandic examples show the relevance of the SOURCE notion, which explains the contrast between (9) and (10).

(9) Hann$_i$ sagdi ad sig$_i$ vantadi hafileika
    he$_i$ said that self$_i$ lacked ability
    'He said that he lacked ability'

(10) *Honum$_i$ var sagt ad sig$_i$ vantadi hafileika
    he$_i$ was told that self$_i$ lacked ability
    'He was told that he lacked ability'

The logophoric element *sig* must refer to the entity which is marked at the discourse level as SOURCE. The semantics of the verb of saying *sagdi* is such that its subject is represented in the discourse as the SOURCE. In terms of File Cards, we can assume that the card representing NP *hann* in (9) is marked as the SOURCE (it also has some number, say #1):

```
  Hann
  #1
  SOURCE
```

If *sig* has an index distinct from that of *hann*, the rules of index translation introduced in Chapter II will require that this NP be represented in the discourse by a file card with a number distinct from the number of *hann*. Given that different file cards represent different individuals (*modulo* bridging possibilities which are not relevant in this example), *sig* will not refer to *hann*, which will violate the requirement that *sig* refers to the SOURCE. Thus, the coindexation of *sig* with *hann* is required but, crucially, not because of syntactic constraints but because of the constraints on establishing reference in the discourse. Using the terminology adopted in this book, *sig* will be incorporated into the card representing *hann*.

Analogously, in (10), *sig* cannot be coindexed with *honum* because the coindexation is translated from syntax into discourse as a representation by the same file card. But the card representing *honum* is not marked as the SOURCE in this case, thus *sig* cannot be represented by the same card and the coindexation is impossible.[33]

The relevance of the notion of PIVOT for the interpretation of logophors is illustrated by the distribution of Japanese *zibun*. A detailed discussion of this element and the role of the discourse in its interpretation can be found in Kuno (1972). Here, I provide just two examples from Sells (1987) that illustrate its discourse properties.

(11) Takasi$_i$ wa [Yosiko ga zibun$_i$ o tazunete-kita node] uresigatta.
 Takasi$_i$ Top [Yosiko Subj self$_i$ Obj visit-came because] happy
 'Takasi$_i$ was happy because Yosiko came to visit him$_i$.'

(12) ?*Takasi$_i$ wa [Yosiko ga zibun$_i$ o tazunete-itta node] uresigatta.
 Takasi$_i$ Top [Yosiko Subj self$_i$ Obj visit-went because] happy
 'Takasi$_i$ was happy because Yosiko went to visit him$_i$.'

As Sells points out, "The PIVOT is understood as the locus to which deictic elements must refer, which explains why pattern of deixis in these examples should be the wau it is..." (p. 465). The difference in the semantics of *come* and *go* is that *come* indicates the motion towards the individual represented as the PIVOT. Given that *Takasi* in the above examples is the individual in relation to whose location the motion is evaluated, *zibun* must be coindexed with *Takasi* because only in this case will it be represented in the discourse by a file card marked as the PIVOT with some number, say #2.

```
┌─────────────────────┐
│  Takasi             │
│                     │
│  #2                 │
│            PIVOT    │
└─────────────────────┘
```

zibun thus will be incorporated into the card representing *Takasi*.

It is important to understand that logophoric elements do not necessarily have to have a morphology different from other pronominals. Clearly, some languages (such as Abe, Mundang, Tikar and other African languages) have developed a morphologically rich system of pronominal elements where logophors have a distinct morphology. But in principle, this is not a universal requirement. One and the same pronominal element can function either as a syntactic reflexive (that is subject to syntactic constraints), or as a logophor (that is referring to a particular discourse role). The case in mind is, of course, English where reflexives *himself/herself* can function either as syntactic, or logophoric elements. The necessity for the coindexation of *himself* with the subject in a sentence like 'Max like himself' is straightforward and explainable in purely syntactic terms. Consider now (13) from Reinhart and Reuland (1993).

(13) Max_i boasted that the queen invited Lucie and $himself_i$ to the tea.

Since *Max* and *himself* are not co-arguments of the same predicate, the reflexive is logophoric. Let us assume that *himself* here refers to the SELF, that is to the one whose mental state or attitude the content of the proposition describes, presumably Max. The syntactic co-indexation of the two NPs will then be translated into the discourse as the incorporation of the card representing NP *himself* into the card representing the SELF, that is Max. The reflexive *himself*, therefore, will be correctly interpreted as referring to Max. But, crucially, unlike the syntactic interpretation of a reflexive, establishing reference for the same element used logophorically requires accessing the discourse level and determining which NP has a specific discourse function, in this case the SELF.

Normal adult speakers are able to carry out both syntactic and discourse-related operations. Establishing reference for either syntactic or logophoric elements, therefore, does not present any problem for these speakers. With regard to children's interpretation of logophors, however, one may predict that they will make more errors interpreting these elements than interpreting purely syntactic reflexives that do not require the discourse level to be accessed. This is so because, as argued in previous chapters, discourse-related operations may require additional processing resources, as they implicate *conversation-internal*, rather than *speaker-internal knowledge*. In fact, there is some evidence that this is, indeed, the case.

In fact there is evidence from the acquisition research on Icelandic that logophors can, indeed, be problematic for young children (see Sigurjonsdottir and Hyams 1992 for the relevant data and analyses along the lines of Reinhart and Reuland's reflexivity theory).

To test this hypothesis with English-speaking children (and with a test battery different from that used by Sigurjonsdottir and Hyams), Jennifer Cunningham and I conducted two experiments, which will be discussed in the following sections. In the first experiment, we investigated children's interpretation of reflexives that are part of a prepositional phrase, and in the second experiment we investigated children's interpretation of reflexives that are part of a "picture NP". The rationale for these experiments is provided below.

2. Locative PPs and "Picture NPs"

According to Marantz (1984), complements of locative prepositions such as *around, behind, near* receive their theta-roles (and case) directly from the preposition. In (14) and (15), for example, reflexives *himself* and *herself* are theta-marked by *near* and *around*, respectively.

(14) Max$_i$ saw a gun near himself$_i$

(15) Mary$_i$ drew a circle around herself$_i$

The antecedents of these reflexives (*Max* and *Mary*, respectively) receive their theta-roles externally from the main predicate. This means that the antecedent and the reflexive are not co-arguments of the same predicate. In the Reflexivity theory, then, these reflexives are not subject to the constraints of the Binding Theory and the distribution of the reflexives is determined by some discourse-related constraints on the interpretation of logophors.

It is interesting that adult speakers are certainly unaware that the mechanisms involved in the interpretation of the reflexive in (14) and (15) and the interpretation of a reflexive in (16) are qualitatively different. In both cases they will identify the reflexive as referring to the matrix subject. But from the theoretical point of view, the mechanisms responsible for these interpretations are different: syntactic in (16) and discourse-related in (14) and (15).

(16) John washed himself.

In fact, it is not entirely clear what discourse mechanisms are involved in the interpretation of the reflexive in (14) and (15). Reinhart and Reuland, who argue for the non-syntactic nature of the anaphoric dependency in these cases do not provide a detailed explanation, stating simply that the mechanism has something to do with the discourse. It is not immediately clear how to describe this dependency in terms of Sell's notions of the SOURCE, SELF, and PIVOT. But for the purposes of this study, we can assume that the exact nature of the logophoric interpretation is not crucial. Let us assume that the logophoric element in these cases receives its reference from the center of discourse using this notion in a more or less intuitive sense. For example, in (17), where there are two potential antecedents for the reflexive, it will be assumed that the center of the discourse coincides with the notion of the topic, which, in turn, is normally represented by the syntactic subject.

(17) [The man near [the boy]$_j$]$_i$ drew a circle around himself$_{i/*j}$.

Thus, NP *The man near the boy*, not NP *the boy*, will be interpreted as the antecedent for the reflexive *himself*. Crucially, however, this interpretation is due to the discourse-related, not a syntactic, mechanism: the subject is interpreted as the (weak) topic, and the topic is interpreted as the center of the discourse. The file card representing [NPThe man....] will be marked as the center of the discourse. Thus, the syntactic coindexation of *himself* with [NPThe man...] is required because only in this case will *himself* be incorporated into the card representing [NPThe man....], which means that *himself* refers to the center of the discourse. To summarise: the coindexation of the reflexive and the subject in (17) is required because of the discourse-related, non-syntactic, constraints on the interpretation of a logophor.

| Man near #4 |
| #3 |
| CENTER |
| Himself |

| The Boy |
| #4 |

Needless to say, the morphological identity of syntactic and logophoric reflexives makes it more difficult to provide a detailed, non-*ad hoc* theory of logophoricity. The distinction may appear to be completely unfounded. An anonymous review, for example, came up with the following discourse in which the reflexive should be able to, but does not, receive its reference extra-sententially:

> Fred really liked to stand in the middle of circles. But John was the only one who was allowed to play with crayons, and John was asleep. Fred had an idea. He put a crayon in John's hand and dragged John over to the middle of the room. Then Fred carefully pulled John around in a circle in such a way that the crayon was touching the floor. Fred was delighted with the result. John had unknowingly drawn a circle around himself.

As the reviewer correctly points out, even in this context, where Fred is clearly the center of the discourse, *himself* cannot refer to *Fred*.

At the same time, some native speakers of American English find a contrast between (18) and (17) (I have changed the gender of the first NP to make the example clearer):

(18) ?? Instead of drawing a circle around the boy's father, the woman near the boy$_i$ drew a circle around himself$_i$.

The new context made NP *the boy* a more prominent discourse entity, and therefore, a more plausible antecedent for the logophoric reflexive. Crucially, this manipulation is possible only for logophoric reflexives. In (19), *himself* cannot refer to *the boy*, although it has been made a more prominent discourse entity:

(19) *Instead of washing the boy's father, the woman near the boy$_i$ washed himself$_i$.

The reflexive here is a co-argument with the subject and therefore its distribution is regulated by the syntactic Condition A. Discourse manipulations are unable to save the syntactically ungrammatical structure.

The point of these examples, actually, is that the distribution of logophors is still an open issue. Judgements seem to be vague, and so is the theory. Psycholinguistic research in this case becomes even more important as it may be able to contribute to the linguistic theory when its usual database (native judgements) do not provide sufficient evidence. The study reported here attempted to do precisely this: to see whether children's responses to sentences with (what is claimed to be) logophoric reflexives differ from their responses to "syntactic reflexives" conditions.

Another case when two apparently identical constructions involve qualitatively different interpretative mechanisms are represented by the so-called "picture NPs." The phrase *take a picture* has two meanings in English. The first, as shown in sentence (20), uses the verb "take" in the canonical sense of "acquire, obtain, select, carry away":

(20) Sally took a picture of Elvis, but left the picture of the Beatles on the dining room table.

The second, (21), uses the verb idiomatically, meaning "to photograph":

(21) Sally took a picture of Elvis, but it came out blurry because she didn't use the proper film.

In the first instance, the verb phrase consists of the verb *take* plus the internal argument, which is the NP *a picture*. In this construction, the PP *of Elvis* is an argument of the NP *picture* rather than of the verb itself. However, when the phrase *take a picture* is used to mean "photograph", it is the PP *of Elvis*, and all its component parts, that comprises the argument of the verb (see Chomsky 1986.) Thus, by varying semantically the meaning of the phrase *take a picture* and inserting anaphors to fill the NP roles, it is possible to construct minimally contrastive sentences, with the sole variation being the argument structure of the verb. This minimal pair is illustrated in (22) with two possible readings given in (a) and (b).

(22) Sally took a picture of herself
   a) Sally 'grabbed' a picture of Sally.
   b) Sally photographed Sally.

When the context specifies the first, literal meaning of the verb *take*, the reflexive is interpreted logophorically because it is not a co-argument with its antecedent. When the context specifies the idiomatic reading, the reflexive is a co-argument with the subject and therefore its interpretation is determined by Principle A of the Binding Theory, that is by a purely syntactic mechanism. Once again, adult speakers are not aware of this difference. In both cases, they correctly interpret the reflexive as referring to the subject of the sentence, although in the first case the mechanism is discourse-related, while in the second the mechanism is syntactic in nature.

Let us assume again that the logophoric reflexive in "picture NP" also refers to the center of discourse. Thus, in a sentence with two potential antecedents for the reflexive, as in (23) below where the literal, "to grab" meanings intended, the reflexive will be interpreted as referring to the subject.

(23) [The woman near [the girl]$_j$]$_i$ took a picture of [herself]$_i$

Similar to the interpretation of logophors in locative PPs, the file card representing NP [the woman near the girl] will be marked as the center of the discourse. Thus, the coindexation of *herself* with the subject is necessary because of the discourse-related, non-syntactic requirements.

As mentioned above, adult speakers are not aware of the different nature of the two mechanisms involved in the interpretation of reflexives in the above examples. Whether the mechanism is syntactic (reflexives as co-arguments), or discourse-related (logophors), they correctly interpret these elements as referring to the subject. Children's performance, on the other hand, is predicted to be different in these two cases. If, as argued in previous chapters, their difficulties are related to the discourse level, not to syntax, one should expect a significantly better performance on constructions of type (16) than on constructions of type (14) and (15). Children are also expected to make fewer errors on "picture NP" sentences when the context specifies the literal reading of the verb *take* than when the interpretation is idiomatic (*to photograph*). These predictions were tested in the following two experiments.

3. General Method

Subjects. Twenty-one pre-schoolers (mean age = 4 years, 2 months; age range=3 years, 5 months to 4 years, 9 months) participated as subjects; ten were female and eleven male. Subjects were students in two preschool classrooms in Saratoga Springs, New York. All were monolingual English speakers.

Design/General Method. The study consisted of two experiments which utilised a modified version of the truth-value judgement task (Crain and McKee, 1985). Each child was seen individually, in a room adjacent to the main preschool classroom, for two sessions lasting approximately fifteen minutes each. Experiment One, which compared children's performance on interpreting reflexives in syntactic argument positions and non-argument (locative PP) positions, was presented in both of the sessions, which were approximately two months apart. Experiment Two, which tested the difference in comprehension between sentences that each contained the verb phrase *take a picture*, which has variable argument structure depending upon its intended meaning, was conducted just subsequent to the second session of Experiment One. For each session, the child was shown pictures and told to listen carefully to the sentence (Experiment One) or story (Experiment Two) that went along with the pictures. At the end of each sentence or story, a puppet (Bert from Sesame Street) would describe what he thought was depicted in the picture. The children were told to reward Bert by giving him his teddy bear to hug if he said something right (something that was happening in the picture), and to give Bert a shoe if he said something wrong (something that was not happening in the picture).

3. 1. Experiment 1: Reflexives in Locative PPs

Materials. The stimuli consisted of six test sentences and eight filler sentences. The test sentences each contained an anaphor with two possible referents. For example, the sentence *The man near the boy is washing himself*, presents a choice of two possible antecedents, the true referent, *man*, and the false referent, *boy*. Each test sentence was presented two times, once with a "true" picture (e.g., the man washing himself while the boy looks on) and once with a "false" picture (the man washing the boy.) The test pictures were drawings of adults and children (either a man and a boy or a woman and a girl), with the adults performing various actions either on themselves (true condition) or on the children (false condition). Half of the test sentences represented necessarily transitive verbs (*wash, cover, tickle*) which would require an anaphor in the coargument position to be correctly interpreted as reflexive. The other three test sentences contained logophoric reflexive pronouns as the objects of prepositional phrases (*hide a book behind, draw a circle around, put a hat on*) in true and false conditions. A complete list of test sentences is shown below in Table 1.

Co-Argument Anaphors (Type A)	Logophors (Type L)
The man near the boy is washing himself.	The man near the boy hid a book behind himself.
The woman near the girl is tickling herself.	The woman near the girl drew a circle around herself.
The woman near the girl covered herself.	The man near the boy put a hat on himself.

Table 1: Test sentences, Experiment One.

Design. As stated above, each of the six test sentences contained either a co-argument anaphor (hereafter referred to as Argument [type A] sentences) or an anaphor in logophoric position (Logophoric [type L] sentences). Each was presented two times, once in a true condition (correctly describing the associated picture) and once in a false condition (incorrectly describing the associated picture). Thus the true/false distinction was within subjects, as was the distinction for type of anaphor (A vs. L).

Procedure. Each child was "trained" to give the puppet the appropriate prop (teddy bear for "true", shoe for "false" using four-to-six modelling sentences. Immediately after this "training", the experimental sentences were presented, interspersed with filler pictures and filler sentences, such as *The boy on the swing is wearing a red hat,* which the children were also asked to judge whether the puppet's description was correct. These fillers were inserted to avoid systematic *yes* or *no* responses and to provide a way for the experimenter to judge if the child was still engaged in the task. Children received no feedback on the test sentences and were never told if their responses were right or wrong. In session one, a total of twenty-three children were tested; however, only twenty-one of these were seen again in session two, and the other two children were eliminated from the sample. Session one consisted of 15 pictures and sentences (8 test sentences and 7 fillers); in session two, the children were presented with 8 sentences (4 tests and 4 fillers).

Coding. The responses were immediately coded by the experimenter. Responses were recorded as correct when the child accepted the true sentences and rejected the false sentences, and incorrect in all other instances. In cases where a child asked clarification questions (e.g., "Washed whoself?") this was noted, but

	Tickle		Cover		Wash		Put hat on		Draw circle		Hide book		Total Synt.		Total Logoph.	
Subj.	T	F	T	F	T	F	T	F	T	F	T	F	T	F	T	F
1(f)	0	0	0	0	0	0	0	0	0	1	0	0	0	0	0	1
2(f)	0	0	0	1	0	0	0	1	0	1	0	1	0	1	0	3
3(m)	0	0	0	1	0	0	0	0	0	1	1	0	0	1	1	1
4(m)	0	0	1	0	0	0	0	1	0	1	0	0	1	0	0	2
5(f)	0	0	0	1	0	0	0	1	0	0	0	0	0	1	0	1
6(f)	0	0	0	0	0	0	0	1	0	1	0	1	0	0	0	3
7(m)	0	0	0	1	0	1	0	1	0	1	0	1	0	2	0	3
8(m)	0	0	0	0	0	0	0	0	0	0	0	1	0	0	0	1
9(m)	0	1	0	0	0	0	0	0	0	0	0	1	0	1	0	1
10(m)	0	0	0	1	0	0	0	1	0	1	0	1	0	1	0	3
11(m)	0	1	0	0	0	0	0	0	0	0	0	0	0	0	0	0
12(m)	0	0	1	1	0	0	0	0	1	0	0	0	1	1	1	0
13(m)	0	0	0	0	0	0	0	0	0	1	1	1	0	0	1	2
14(f)	0	0	0	0	0	0	0	1	0	1	0	0	0	0	0	2
15(f)	0	0	1	1	0	0	0	1	0	1	0	0	1	1	0	2
16(f)	0	0	0	1	0	0	0	0	0	1	0	0	0	1	0	1
17(f)	0	0	0	0	0	1	0	1	0	1	0	0	0	1	0	2
18(m)	0	0	0	0	0	0	0	0	0	1	0	0	0	0	0	1
19(m)	0	0	0	1	0	0	0	0	0	1	0	1	0	1	0	2
20(f)	0	0	0	0	0	0	0	0	0	1	0	1	0	0	0	2
21(f)	0	0	0	0	0	0	0	0	0	1	0	0	0	0	0	1
Tot.	0	2	3	9	0	2	0	9	1	16	2	9	3	13	3	34

Table 2: Errors per child, Experiment One.

his/her final response was what was used for coding purposes.

Predictions. Previous studies described in previous chapters showed that children are able to interpret pronominals whose interpretation requires solely syntactic knowledge before they can utilise the associated discourse principles. Thus, we ought to expect an analogous result for anaphors. If reflexive anaphors outside the argument structure of the verb are truly outside the scope of the Binding Theory, then children should make mistakes in judging sentences containing these phrases even after they have mastered syntactic constraints on the distribution of reflexives.

Results. The data for Experiment one are summarised in Tables 2 (above) and 3 (below). Table 2 shows the errors per child. Table 3 shows the total number of errors (false acceptances or true rejections) for each truth condition of each type of sentence (syntactic-argument vs. logophoric reflexive).

	%True	%False
Argument	5	21
Logophoric	5	54

Table 3: %Total errors per condition, Experiment One.

As expected, following the results of Chien and Wexler (1990), Padilla (1990), Grimshaw and Rosen (1990), and Avrutin and Wexler (1992), the children made fewer errors in the true condition than in the false condition, falsely accepting anaphors in the place of pronouns. This is at least partially due to the fact that, as Grimshaw and Rosen point out, children have a general tendency to answer "yes" when asked if something an adult has said is acceptable.

The children made errors in interpreting the six anaphors in argument position (syntactic reflexives) in 16 of 126 instances, or 13% of the time. Thirteen of these errors (81%) were false acceptances. Children had a much more difficult time with logophoric reflexives, with a 29% error rate (37 of 126). Within the false condition of Type L anaphors, performance was basically at chance (53% error). This difference in performance between syntactic and logophoric reflexives was analysed using a two-factor ANOVA and found to be quite significant [$F(1, 20)=11.65, p < .001$]. The difference in performance between true and false sentences also yielded a very significant main effect [$F(1, 20)=44.20, p < .001$] and logophors, and, across all conditions, the children had by far the most trouble rejecting false sentences containing logophors.

The subjects' total errors were distributed evenly throughout each verb of each particular type, with one very noticeable exception: the verb *cover* was responsible for twelve of the sixteen errors in the syntactic reflexive test sentences. In addition, the two pictures associated with this verb seemed to draw more commentary from the children; one girl insisted that the woman was *uncovering* rather than covering the girl. ("No, see? She took the blanket off the girl."). These two *cover* pictures were dissimilar to all other pictures used in that they were pen-and-ink drawings rather than colored pictures. For whatever reason, performance on each of the two *cover* sentences was markedly worse than on either of its syntactic-argument condition counterparts *wash* and *tickle*. If we assume something was anomalous for these two sentences and temporarily exclude them from our analysis, the results are even stronger (see Table 4), with a new significance level of $F(1, 61)=29.07, p < .001$.

	%True	%False
Argument	0	4
Logophoric	3	34

Table 4: %Total errors per condition, Experiment One, without *cover*

Discussion. Results of Experiment 1 show quite clearly that children make more errors with logophoric reflexives than with syntactic. How can we explain this pattern of responses in terms of incorrect use if indices and file cards adopted in this book for the experimental results with pronouns?

First, children's near perfect performance with syntactic reflexives mirrors their responses to sentences with pronouns bound by quantified antecedents, as in (24) and (25).

(24) Every bear washed him.
(25) Who washed him?

As argued above, only syntactic mechanisms (e.g. Condition B) are involved in this case and children demonstrate near adult performance. Similarly, their good performance in sentences with syntactic reflexives demonstrate their full mastery of the syntactic Condition A of the Binding Theory. In fact, this result is a replication of a well-established result on children's knowledge of Condition A discussed in previous chapters.

Children's poor performance with logophoric reflexives mirrors their performance on sentences with pronouns and R-expression antecedents, as in (26).

(26) Father Bear washed him.

In Chapter III, I gave analyses of these results in terms of an incorrect use of indexation. I argued that children allow two NPs to have different indices but still refer to the same individual. Consider now one of the experimental sentences repeated here as (27).

(27) [The man near [the boy]$_j$]$_i$ drew a circle around himself$_{i/*j}$.

Since the reflexive is not a co-argument with its antecedent in this case, there are no *syntactic* conditions on the possible pattern of indexation. The existing restrictions are discourse-related: *himself* must be coindexed with the center of discourse. As in Chapter III, we continue to assume that when children are presented with a picture and a sentence, they try to find some grammatical representation of the sentence that would be true of the picture (in other words, children try to accept the sentence as an accurate description of the situation). Suppose children are shown a "true" picture, that is a picture where the man has drawn a circle around himself. Syntactic conditions do not prohibit the co-indexation of the reflexive with the subject (in fact, they do not prohibit any co-indexation). Nor are any discourse-related constraints violated in this case: NP *himself* will be incorporated in the discourse into the card representing NP *The man...*, which is marked as the center of the discourse. Thus, all conditions will be satisfied and children can safely say "Yes" to this sentence. As we can see from the experimental results, they indeed make very few errors in the "True" condition. It should be pointed out, that this result is parallel to the results obtained by Grimshaw and Rosen (1990) who report that children almost always correctly accept sentences that are true descriptions of the presented pictures.

Suppose now children are shown a "false" picture", that is a picture where the man has drawn a circle around the boy. To accept the sentence as a true description, speakers have to have a discourse representation where *himself* is incorporated into the card representing *the boy*, which means that the two NPs must co-indexed in syntax. Again, syntactic constraints are irrelevant and such a co-indexation is allowed from the syntactic point of view. But it is not allowed (for adult speakers) from the discourse perspective: the card representing NP *the boy* is not marked as the center of discourse. Suppose, however, that, in their attempt to accept a sentence, children will try to make changes in their discourse representation, specifically, to "mark" the card representing NP *the boy* as the center of discourse. For adult speakers, this change is not allowed unless there are special discourse conditions such as, for example, in (18) above. Moreover, recall our discussion of the File Change Semantics. Files represent a common ground of conversation, that is something that represents mutual knowledge of the participants in a given conversation. As a common ground, individual files cannot be changed without informing other participants about these changes. In other words, if children attempt to make this change in their discourse representation, they need to make sure that other participants in the conversation will make corresponding changes as well. This means that children need to take into account other speakers' files (to access their discourse representations). As I suggested in Chapter III for the interpretation of pronouns, this operation may require additional resources and children, therefore, may make errors. Specifically, they may allow "individual" changes in their discourse representations (such as marking of NP *the boy* as the center of discourse) without correct accessing other speakers' files and realising that this change is not mirrored in other files. As a result, children sometimes will say "Yes" to the "False" condition allowing the logophoric reflexive to refer to what adult speakers take to be a less discourse prominent entity.

Thus, similar to the incorrect interpretation of pronouns in sentences of type (26), children's errors with logophoric reflexives are due to the discourse-related constraints. Somewhat similar claim regarding temporal anaphora (to which I return in Chapter VIII) was made in Hyams 1996, who argues that some structures "...are felicitous in a broader set of pragmatic circumstances in the child's grammar than in the adult's due to the absence or inaccessibility..." of a specific discourse-related constraint. This claim is certainly applicable to the case of logophoric reflexives: as we saw in (18), under specific discourse conditions, adult speakers will also allow the coreference of *himself* and *the boy*. According to Hyams, children's pragmatics is "freer" and such a coreference is allowed even without overt changes in the discourse.

Although I agree with Hyams' claim, I propose that these restrictions are due to the general limitations on processing resources, which are characteristic of children. As above, certain similarities between children and brain-damaged patients seem to support this processing account of errors.

Finally, it should be noted that similar results were reported by Padilla (1990) for Spanish speaking children. Although Padilla did not specifically attempt to investigate children's knowledge of logophors, some of his results can be interpreted as supporting the claim that children have more difficulties with logophoric reflexives than with syntactic. He found that "...children gave less disjoint reference responses for reflexives in S [i.e. bound by the subject of the same clause, S.A.] than within PP, and conversely more coreference within S than in PP. Thus, reflexives within PP are more problematic for younger children (3- and 5-year-olds) than reflexives within S. The results reflect a tendency to treat reflexives within PP as pronouns, especially at early developmental stages" (p. 139).

In fact, these results can be reinterpreted as supporting the claim that children's difficulties are due to the discourse-related, rather than syntactic constraints: Spanish-speaking children made significantly more errors interpreting logophoric than syntactic reflexives.

We turn now to Experiment 2 that investigated children's knowledge of reflexives in "Picture NPs."

3.2 Experiment Two: Reflexives in "Picture NPs"

Materials/Design. As discussed above, the phrase *take a picture* has two meanings in English. The first, as shown in sentence (28), uses the verb "take" in the canonical sense of "acquire, obtain, select, carry away":

(28) Sally took a picture of herself, but left the picture of the Beatles on the dining room table.

The second, (29), uses the verb idiomatically, meaning "to photograph":

(29) Sally took a picture of herself, but it came out blurry because she didn't use the proper film.

The important difference between the two readings is that only in (29) are *Sally* and *herself* co-arguments, and therefore *herself* is subject to the syntactic constraint on the distribution of reflexives. In (28) they are not; *Sally* is an argument of *took* while *herself* is an argument of *picture*.

To establish an appropriate context so that one semantic interpretation was favored over another, four stories of 6-12 sentences each were constructed: one for the true and false conditions of each possible interpretation of the phrase *take a picture*: "photograph" (syntactic) and "select" (logophoric), with one illustration representing each story. As in Experiment One, each test sentence contained two possible referents for the anaphor. Here is an example of a true condition with a non-coargument reflexive.

Sample story ('select' = non-coargument, true): Once upon a time there was a man who had a funny hobby. He liked collecting pictures. He had a lot of pictures, his own pictures, and pictures of his friends, too. He kept them in different boxes, so here he kept his own pictures, and here he kept all the pictures of his sister, and here he kept all the pictures of his friend the clown.

So, once he invited his friend the clown to his house for dinner. The man said, "I've got lots of pictures of you, and of other people too. You see, all your pictures are in this box, and all my pictures are in this one. You know, I wanna do something nice for you. If you want, you can choose any picture you like and take it home."

The clown said, "Wow, that's terrific, thanks! You know, I think I look really cool here, so I'll take one of my own pictures, this one. I'll put it on the wall in my bedroom."

Bert: The clown next to the man took a picture of himself.

Procedure. The stories were presented as Truth-Value judgement tasks as in Experiment One. The experimenter held up a picture illustrating each story and read the story carefully to each child, pointing out the various characters as she went. Immediately following each story, the puppet uttered a test sentence summarising what he believed had taken place. The children were once again asked to "reward" the puppet with a teddy bear for a correct answer and a shoe for a false answer. Due to the longer length of these stories as opposed to the test sentences of Experiment One, no filler sentences were used; instead, the children were asked to point at certain characters or events in the picture as the story was read to ensure that their interest was held.

Coding. As in Experiment One, the subjects' responses were immediately coded by the experimenter. Responses were considered correct when the child accepted the true sentences and rejected the false sentences, and incorrect in the case of an incorrect response or no response.

Subject	Argument		Non-argument	
	T	F	T	F
1 (F)	0	1	1	1
2 (F)	0	0	0	0
3 (M)	0	0	0	0
4 (M)	0	0	1	0
5 (F)	0	0	1	0
6 (F)	0	0	1	0
7 (M)	0	1	0	1
8 (M)	0	0	1	1
9 (M)	0	1	0	1
10 (M)	0	0	1	1
11 (M)	0	0	1	1
12 (M)	0	1	0	1
13 (M)	0	0	0	0
14 (F)	0	1	0	0
15 (F)	0	0	0	0
16 (F)	0	0	0	1
17 (F)	0	0	1	0
18 (M)	0	0	0	0
19 (M)	0	0	0	1
20 (F)	0	0	0	1
21 (F)	0	0	0	0
TOTAL	**0**	**5**	**8**	**10**

Table 5: Errors per child, Experiment Two

Results. The children made errors in 5 of 42 (12%) sentences containing anaphors within PPs in syntactic-argument positions (*take a picture* = "photograph"); this is once again markedly better than their performance in interpreting PPs containing logophors (*take a picture* = "select a picture"), where they made errors in 18 of 42 cases (43%). The data, summarised in Tables 5 and 6 below, show a main effect of a high error rate in both instances where anaphors occurred in non-argument positions. As in Experiment One, this difference was quite significant in a two-factor ANOVA [$F(1,20)=12.085$, $p < .001$]. However, due to a relatively high number of rejections of true sentences in the non-argument condition (8 of 21, or 38%), the p-value for truth value approached, but did not reach, significance [$p=0.066$]. The interaction was also not significant [$p=0.42$].

Discussion. Overall results of Experiment 2 replicate results of Experiment 1. Children made significantly more errors in those cases when a reflexive is not a co-argument with the subject, that is when it is interpreted logophorically. Interestingly, the sentences presented to children in this experiment were (superficially) absolutely identical. The only difference was in the grammatical analyses assigned to this sentence in different conditions. Children demonstrated that they are sensitive to this variation: as in Experiment 1, when the interpretation of the reflexive required non-syntactic mechanisms, they made more errors. The analyses of these errors are parallel to the analyses of errors in Experiment 1. I propose that children incorrectly allowed marking of a less prominent NP in the discourse as the center, which led some of them to the non-adult interpretation of the reflexive.

Argument (syntactic)	12
Non-argument (logophoric)	42

Table 6: % of Total Errors, Experiment Two

	True	False
Argument (syntactic)	0	24
Non-argument (logophoric)	38	48

Table 7: % of Errors per Condition, Experiment Two

As we can see from Table 7, however, results of Experiment 2 differ from the results of Experiment 1 in the unexpectedly high percentage of incorrect rejections of a true sentence (38% in Experiment 2 vs. 5% in Experiment 1). Although it was predicted that children would make errors in the logophoric condition, it is not clear why they should say "NO" to the sentence correctly describing the picture, and, in particular, why this result showed up only in Experiment 2.

The answer to this puzzle is not entirely clear at the moment. One possibility is that the way of presenting target sentences was somewhat different in Experiment 2. The sentence followed a story which described a chain of events. It is possible that, at least for some children, the story made the second character (e.g. the man in the sample story above) somehow more discourse prominent. In this case, some children may have marked the file card representing this NP as the center of discourse, which resulted in their rejection of the coreferential interpretation of the reflexive with the subject. A more detailed answer requires further investigation.

4. Conclusions

In this chapter, I have discussed results of two experiments that aimed at investigating children's knowledge of the distribution of logophoric reflexives in English. The most important result of these two experiments is that children make significantly more errors with logophoric than with syntactic reflexives. That these results were obtained with English-speaking children is especially interesting because in this language the morphological form of the two types of reflexives are identical. That is, one and the same element can be interpreted either by syntactic or by discourse-related mechanisms. As I argued in this book, discourse-related mechanisms are "more expensive", that is, they require additional resources for their implementation. Assuming that children lack these resources, their poor performance with logophoric reflexives (as well as with pronouns in sentences with R-expression antecedents) is predicted.

The results reported in this chapter support the general claim of this book, specifically, that children possess, and are able to implement, the relevant syntactic knowledge. Their difficulties are argued to lie in a non-syntactic domain, in particular in the domain of the discourse. In the next chapter, I turn to an apparently different phenomenon in child grammar, which, as I will try to demonstrate, can find an explanation along the same line adopted in previous chapters: availability of syntactic knowledge, and difficulties with the syntax-discourse interface. This phenomenon is known as Optional Infinitives.

CHAPTER VIII

DISCOURSE-BASED ANALYSES OF ROOT INFINITIVES

In this chapter, I turn to another error observed in the speech of children and Broca's aphasics, namely the incorrect use of untensed clauses[34]. It has been reported that children acquiring many languages (crucially, non-pro-drop languages, see discussion below) allow the verb to be untensed (that is, Root Infinitives, such as *Michel dormir* 'Michel sleep' in French, or *Mommy go*, in English.) I provide syntactic and discourse analyses of these constructions and argue that, similar to the errors discussed in previous chapters, root infinitives can also be explained on the assumption of the limited processing resources, although with a certain modification of this hypothesis.

I begin with the question, whether Root Infinitives (RIs) widely observed in child speech are consistent with the principles of Universal Grammar, and if so, whether we can find similar constructions in adult languages. If these constructions indeed exist in adult language (or some registers), the question is whether it is possible to analyse them in the same way as children's RIs.

As in the case of logophoric reflexives, discussed in the previous chapter, a detailed theory of discourse processes involved in the interpretation of Root Infinitives remains to be developed. In this chapter I will simply demonstrate that these constructions are grammatical in adult language, although their use is restricted to specific registers. The matter of when speakers actually use these registers is beyond the scope of this work. But, in fact, it should not prevent one from attempting to provide linguistic analyses of these constructions. The situation is similar to the so-called "diary" register of English. It is well known that English, which is not a pro-drop language, allows null subjects in some specific contexts, such as diaries: "Got up at 7. Took shower. Had breakfast. Left." The question of when this register is used appears to be irrelevant for providing linguistic analyses of the null subject phenomenon in English. The same is true about Root Infinitives: As will be shown below, analyses of these constructions do not always require a detailed understanding of their use.

The main claim of this chapter, therefore, is that RIs are consistent with the UG and that these constructions can be found in adult grammars as well. Examples that I discuss include Russian Root Infinitives ("Princess sentences"), English Mad Magazine sentences and English headline sentences. Furthermore, I will argue that what all these constructions have in common is a non-syntactic way of introducing event file cards (in terms of Heim 1982) into the discourse. Thus, children's apparently syntactic errors are better characterised as errors related to the discourse level of representation. Finally, providing some data from the speech of brain-damaged patients, I offer an explanation for the existence of these errors in terms of limited processing resources.

1. The Data

Researchers in many languages have noted that young children (approximately 18 - 28 months old) pass through the stage when they incorrectly use infinitives in main clauses. Examples in (1) and (2) illustrate this error.

(1) a. Michelle dormir (French: Pierce 1989)
  Michelle sleep
 b. Pappa schoenen wassen (Dutch: Weverink 1989)
  daddy shoes wash

(2) a. Thorsten das haben (German: Wexler 1994)
  Thorsten that have
 b. Mommy eat cookie (English: Radford 1990)

Most of the previous analyses of the Optional Infinitive (OI) stage in child grammar argued for a syntactic explanation of this non-adult pattern. For example, Lebeaux 1988, Radford 1990, Vainika 1994, Rizzi 1994, among others, proposed that children's syntactic representation of the sentence is incomplete, in the sense that some syntactic projections are missing (IP, or CP, or both). For example, Vainikka 1994 argues that the sentences in (1a-d) should be analysed as VPs with the subject remaining in [Spec, VP].

Another "purely syntactic" account proposed, for example, by Boser et al. 1992, Ingram and Thompson 1996, suggests that the OI sentences represent the case of null modals. Thus, sentences of type (1e), for example, 'Mommy eat cookie', supposedly mean something like 'Mommy must/should/need eat cookie'. Children in this stage optionally drop modals producing structures exemplified in (1a-d).

Most recently, Wexler (1995) proposed a new syntactic account of the Optional Infinitive stage. Wexler argues for a somewhat modified version of the "incomplete tree" account. Specifically, he suggests that the child syntactic representation lacks the TP projection. Unlike other theories, however, he argues that the child, in certain cases, *is forced* to delete TP because of the following reasons. First, Wexler adopts Chomsky's (1995) claim that interpretable features (those that must stay until LF) do not delete after checking. In adult grammar, the distinction between interpretable and uninterpretable features is exemplified in the distinction between categorical D feature and Case (the former being interpretable, the latter uninterpretable). Thus, the D feature does not delete after checking, while the Case does. Wexler hypothesises that children can take the D feature to be either [+interp], or [-interp]. In other words, there is a stage when children optionally take the D feature to be *formal*, similar to the Case. DP then raises to check off D-feature of Tense but given that this feature is [-interp] for children, it erases after checking off the D feature of Tense. AgrS, then, is left with its feature unchecked, and the derivation crashes.

(3)

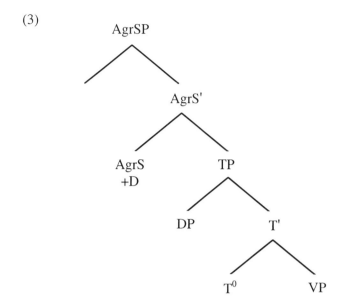

Wexler's important assumption is that to make the derivation converge, children will delete the Tense projection, as in (4).

(4)

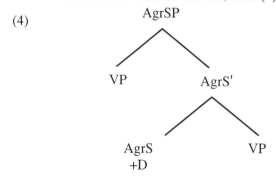

In this case, the derivation converges, but the verb shows up in its infinitival form. Alternatively, if children choose D feature to be [+interp], as in adult grammar, this feature will not delete after checking off the D feature of TENSE, DP will move further up to [Spec, AgrS] to check off its D feature, and the derivation converges in the same way as it does for adults. The verb correctly shows up in its tensed form. Thus, the optionality of the feature specification of D results in the optionality of the verb's infinitival form in the child's speech. Wexler (1995) further shows how this theory explains a wide range of linguistic phenomena in child speech, such as the absence of the OI stage in null subject languages, the absence of infinitives with the verb *be*, default case, and others.

For a more detailed discussion of the first two approaches to the root infinitive phenomenon and criticism of these theories, I refer the reader to Poeppel and Wexler (1993). Regarding Wexler's TP deletion account, it represents a very intriguing possibility, although a number of questions remain open. For example, it is not clear why children allow the incorrect specification of the D feature, and what eventually forces them to switch to the adult interpretation. Also, it is not clear why children choose to delete TP, not AgrS, when forced to do something to save the derivation. Finally, it is not clear why children do not change the value of the D feature from [-interp] to [+interp] when the choice of the former leads to the crash of the derivation.

There is a number of other approaches to children's Root Infinitives (such as Rizzi's 1994 Truncation Hypothesis) which I cannot discuss here. For an excellent summary and a new, morphosyntactic analysis see Phillips 1995, Schaeffer 1997, among others. In the next section, however, I would like to focus a little bit more on the Underspecification Theory proposed by Hyams 1996. The reason is that, as will become clear shortly, Hyams' account is, at least, conceptually close to the theory I will propose in this chapter.

2. Hyams' Underspecification Theory of Root Infinitives

The central claim of Hyams' theory is that Tense in children's syntactic representation can be *underspecified*. More specifically, Hyams argues that T^0 in the child's representation can be left *unindexed*. This representation is different from the adult' for whom T^0 must bear an index. Following Gueron and Hoekstra (1989, 1994), Hyams assumes that T^0 can be either coindexed or contraindexed with the Tense Operator (TO) which forms (through the Comp) a tense chain with T.

CHAPTER VIII

The pattern of T indexation yields the following interpretations (from Hyams 1996):

(5) a. (TO$_i$) John [T$_i$]knows the answer.   Present
    b. (TO$_i$) John [T$_j$] drove his car.   Past

Hyams hypothesises that in the early grammar, T^0 may fail to bear an index:

(6) (TO$_i$) Teddy bear [T$_0$] sleep.

When T^0 is left underspecified (i.e. unindexed), there will be no morphological features realised on the verb, which corresponds to the root infinitive clauses in child speech. An interesting question that Hyams raises at this point is what kind of temporal interoperation children give to these sentences. On the face of it, sentences with underspecified T^0 should have no temporal interpretation at all. At the same time, it has been claimed in the literature (e.g. Kramer 1993) that root infinitives generally denote ongoing events (although Behrens 1994 claims that non-finite forms are used by children in a variety of ways, for all tenses, see below). Hyams assumes that when T^0 is without an index, it somehow receives a present tense, or *here and now interpretation*. Such an interpretation, in Hyams' theory, can be thought of as a case of *temporal coreference* as opposed to the case of *syntactic binding* of T^0 by TO exemplified by (5a). As Hyams points out:

> "Following in the spirit of Partee's proposal [see Partee (1973). S.A.] that the use of Tense parallels that of pronouns, I am suggesting that a present tense T can be either anaphoric ... or it can enter into coreference, in which case there is no binding relation between the operator and T. We thus have temporal anaphora and temporal coreference, analogous nominal anaphora and nominal coreference, as described in Reinhart (1983). Root infinitives involve temporal coreference." (p. 17).

The pattern of indexation proposed by Hyams is also parallel to the pattern proposed by Reinhart for the nominal anaphora: coindexation only means syntactic binding, while non-syntactic, coreferential relation involves no indexation at all. Moreover, as discussed in previous chapters, Reinhart (1983) and Grodzinsky and Reinhart (1993) argue that there is a specific (pragmatic) rule (Rule I) that prohibits a pronominal element from entering a coreference relation with its antecedent if the resulting interpretation would be indistinguishable from the one obtained by the use of the bound variable anaphora. I have already discussed this theory in Chapter III, but to recapitulate the central point, consider (7).

(7) *John$_i$ likes him$_i$.

This sentence is ungrammatical not only because of Principle B which prohibits the coindexation of the pronoun with the subject, but also because of Rule I, which *requires* that the bound variable anaphora (e.g. the coindexation) be used. Syntax rules out the binding relationship, while pragmatics rules out the possibility of coreference. With regard to children, Grodzinsky and Reinhart suggest that Rule I is unavailable (or is not implementable) by them, which may lead to the incorrect interpretation of *him* as coreferential with *John*, a pattern of errors extensively discussed in previous chapters.

Following Reinhart's analyses of syntactic anaphora and coreference, Hyams introduces Rule T, which is meant to parallel Rule I for nominal anaphora. This rule (from Hyams 1996) is given in (8).

(8) **Rule T**
I(nfl) A cannot corefer with I(nfl) B if replacing A with C, C a variable bound by B, yields an indistinguishable interpretation.

Thus, the coindexation of T and TO in (5a) is required when the desired temporal interpretation is Present, and the representation in (6) is blocked because it yields an interpretation obtained in (5a). Furthermore, following Grodzinsky and Reinhart, Hyams suggests that Rule T is either unavailable, or unimplementable by young children. If so, children may sometimes allow (6) as a possible representation with the temporal interpretation of Tense supplied pragmatically as the case of coreference with the *here and now* point of time.

Hyams' theory of the root infinitives in child grammar appears to be precisely on the right track. What I take to be the most important insight of her theory is that the apparently syntactic error (lack of overt tense marking) is analysed as a non-syntactic, pragmatic error. Moreover, Hyams attempts to provide a unified explanation for the two patterns of errors observed in developmental linguistics: incorrect use of pronouns and optional infinitives[35].

In the next sections, I will present what I think is a more detailed theory of the role of discourse in the temporal interpretation of clauses, and more specifically in the errors observed in child speech. But first of all, I will discuss the case of root infinitives in adult grammars. I begin with adult Russian.

3. Root Infinitives in Adult Russian

In this section, I discuss a specific register in adult Russian that allows (under certain conditions) the use of Root Infinitives. It should be noted that a similar construction exists in other languages, for example in Dutch. In this chapter, however, I restrict my discussion to Russian. For the analyses of Dutch RIs the reader is referred to Haegeman 1994. Under normal, unmarked discourse conditions, Russian (like English and other languages) requires that clauses have a syntactic representation of Tense:

(9) a. Ivan begal/begaet/*begat'
Ivan ran/runs/*to-run
b. Carevna xoxotala/xoxočet/*xoxotat'
Princess laughed/laughs/*to-laugh

Infinitival forms of the verb are prohibited by the Case Filter: only tensed Infl assigns Nominative Case to the subject. However, as illustrated in (10) (referred to as "Princess sentences"), Russian does allow root infinitives but under some specific, discourse-related circumstances.

(10) a. Carevna xoxotat'
    princess to-laugh
    'The Princess started to laugh'
    (straight after something funny happened)
   b. Zriteli applodirovat'
    spectators to-applaud
    'The spectators started to applaud'
    (straight after something exciting was done)

Descriptively, these constructions are characterised by several interesting properties. First, in an apparent violation of the Case Filter, the sentences are fully grammatical and productive, although the verb is in its infinitival form, which means that Infl does not assign Case to the subject. Second, the action described by the verb indicates the beginning of an action that follows immediately some event assumed to be known. Third, these constructions impose a referentiality constraint on the subject. As (11) demonstrates, quantifiers are not allowed in the subject position in these constructions:

(11) a. * Nikto ne xoxotat'
    nobody not to-laugh
    'Nobody started to laugh'
   b. ?* Každyj zritel' applodirovat'
    every   spectator to-applaud
    every spectator started to applaud'
   c. * kto xoxotat'?
    who to-laugh
    'Who started to laugh?'

Parallel examples with finite verbs, e.g. (12), are grammatical:

(12) Nikto ne xoxotal/ne načal xoxotat'
   nobody not laughed/not started to-laugh

The following questions arise regarding these constructions. How does the subject receive Nominative Case in these structures? If it does not, how is it possible for the discourse to circumvent the apparently purely syntactic constraint which (used to be) known as the Case Filter? Why are the elements that are interpreted as operators impossible in these constructions? How are these constructions interpreted temporally in the absence of any tense specification? Finally, what are the similarities and differences between these structures and children's optional infinitives?

3.1. The Role of Indices in the Representation of NPs, Tenses and Events

I propose that not only NPs (as in Heim 1982) but also *events* introduce file cards in the discourse representation of a sentence. Contrary to what I suggested in Avrutin 1997, both events and states (or, in terms of Bach 1981, *eventualities*) have corresponding file cards, to which, for simplicity, I will refer as Event File Cards. The fact that clauses involve reference to events has been widely assumed in the literature (e.g. Davidson 1967, Higginbotham 1983, 1985, Bennett 1988, Parsons 1990, Piñon 1996, among others). What is new in my proposal, I believe, is that events have a discourse representation on a par with NPs, and, assuming Heim's 1982 model, are represented in the file through Event File Cards (see, however, Kamp and Reyle 1993 for the DRT-type model of events in discourse.) Thus, the discourse representation of a sentence *John ate an apple* will be as in (13).

(13)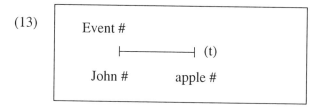

In (13), the Event file card contains a time interval during which the event holds, and two *individual* file cards representing participants in the event. As discussed in Chapter II, the number of these cards are instantiating constants of the variable index on the subject and object NPs. The number of the Event card itself is the instantiating constant of the variable index on the event argument introduced by the predicate. Finally, I hypothesise that in order for a time interval to be specified, T^0 has to have an index, too. More specifically, I propose that T^0 and e must be coindexed at LF in order to derive an interpretation that a certain event holds during some interval of time[36]. As I will show later, the requirement of their coindexation follows from Gueron and Hoekstra's 1995 theory of Tense Chain, according to which T^0 and e are elements of the same chain. As we will see shortly, it might be better to formulate this requirement as a prohibition against contraindexing of T^0 and e, where the absence of an index on one element and the presence of an index on the other counts as contraindexing.

John and *apple* are interpreted as participants in the event of eating due to the semantic representation of the sentence in (14), where S stands for the *speech time*.

(14) $\exists e \exists x$ (eat (e)^Agent (e, John)^Theme (e,x)^apple (x))^e<S$

Both subject and object NPs introduce discourse referents and are interpretable because they are represented by file cards with corresponding numbers, which are contained in the card representing the event[37].

Suppose now that an index on an NP and an index on T^0 are formal expressions of the presence of D feature (Chomsky 1995). The meaning of this feature is that the element bearing it has what I call "Referential Potential." Thus, presence of an index on T^0 means that T^0 has a referential potential and can denote (in principle) a time interval (c.f. Dowty 1979). The presence of an index on an NP means that this NP can (in principle) introduce a discourse referent in the form of an individual file card (i.e. a card representing an individual).

According to Chomsky 1995, this feature must checked off; in other words an NP bearing this feature must be in Spec - Head relation with a head that has a checking capacity (i.e. the relevant featural content). In terms of indexation, this amounts to saying that both NP in Spec, TP and T^0 must bear indices. Thus, in (15), only (c) is a possible representation, which corresponds to a normal Tensed clause in (16)[38]:

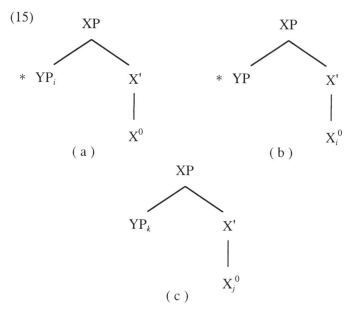

(16) John$_k$ T$_j$ ate(e$_j$) an apple$_m$

The following analyses will crucially rely on adopting Hyams' (1996) proposal that T^0 of an infinitival clause has no index. Intuitively, this claim seems to be correct because infinitival tenses do not denote any time intervals. Thus, I will assume it without further argument.

(17) T^0 of an infinitival clause has no index.

(15a) correctly represents the ungrammatical (18), traditionally ruled out as a violation of the Case Filter:

(18). *John to eat an apple.

I will not discuss the cases corresponding to (15b) in this work. Let me just speculate that (15b) may represent a clause with an expletive subject before Expletive replacement or adjunction of an NP to the expletive at LF (e.g. *There came a knight to the village.*) This will require us to assume that expletives have no referential potential (which seems to be true) and therefore have no D feature and no index. I will not, however, discuss this issue.

Let me turn now to root infinitives (RIs). Represented in (15a), these structures are (in a normal register) ungrammatical. Notice, however, that, formally speaking, there is one more possible pattern of indexation not shown in (15); the one that does not violate the constraint on "asymmetrical" indexation of Spec and Head. This is the case when *neither* Head, *nor* NP in the Specifier position has any index:

(19)

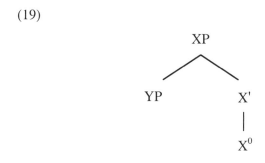

Strictly speaking, (19) does not represent a case of the violation of the indexation requirement; but the corresponding sentences would, of course, be uninterpretable: as T^0 has no index, the event cannot be anchored (in terms of Enç 1987), nor can an NP be interpreted (recall the index on an NP is required to have a number of the corresponding file card.) The event variable in this case will also have to be unindexed since T^0 is unindexed. Thus, (20) is, formally speaking, allowed, but the structure is uninterpretable:

(20) John T^0 (to) leave(e).

My claim is that (19) *is*, in fact, the representation of RIs in certain adult registers, and is allowed, in some cases, by young children. I will argue that these, normally uninterpretable structures, *are* interpreted by a very specific, discourse - related mechanism, to which I turn now.

3.2. Discourse Representation of Russian Root Infinitives

Since e has no index (because T^0 is unindexed), its index cannot be instantiated with a number of an Event file card, representing e in the discourse. Nor can the subject NP have a discourse representation as it lacks an index as well. Thus, apparently, the structure should be uninterpretable.

Suppose, however, that an Event file card (with its components, such as individual cards and the time interval) can be introduced into the discourse by some other means, not through the instantiation of the index of e. In what follows, I will show that there are such ways, which correspond to different instances of Root Infinitives.

I propose that the first way of introducing an Event file card by non-syntactic, discourse - based means is related to the notion of a Resultant (Consequent) State, as discussed in Parsons 1990. Parsons distinguishes between *In-Progress Events* and *Culminated Events* (events that are going on at the relevant moment and events that are completed, or *culminated*.) According to Parsons, only Culminated events (e.g. perfective predicates) introduce in the semantic representation a Resultant State. The logical form of *John has eaten an apple* is given in (21), where CS is a partial function from eventualities to eventualities which assigns each event its consequent (Resultant) state:

(21) $\exists e \exists x$ (eat (e) $\wedge$ Agent (e, John) $\wedge$ Theme (e,x) $\wedge$ apple (x)) $\wedge$ hold(CS(e), S))

The sentence, therefore, contains in its semantic representation an In-Progress event of John eating an apple, its culmination and a resultant state -- a situation where the apple is eaten by John.

Suppose now that in terms of the discourse representation, the difference between the In-Progress and Culminated events is the following. In-Progress events introduce one Event file card (with a number instantiating the variable index on e), while Culminated events introduce two: one corresponding to the event itself (e.g. *John has eaten an apple*), and the other corresponding to the Resultant state. Let us say that the card representing the culminated event *projects* a new card (with some new number). In other words, a new file card, which is necessary for the interpretation, can be introduced in the discourse as a result of a *projection* by another card, representing a culminated event. Let me show now that this is precisely what happens in the case of Russian root infinitives: I will argue that these clauses are represented by the projected event cards.

First of all, notice that the projection is possible *only* in the case of a culminated event because only such an event is associated with a resultant state. Thus, it is predicted that Russian RIs should be possible only if, in the discourse, they follow some other, *necessarily culminated event*. This is, indeed, the case:

(22) a. Korol' rasskazal anekdot. Carevna xoxotat'
King (has) told a joke. Princess to-laugh.

b. Korol' rasskazyval anekdot. *Carevna xoxotat'.
King was telling a joke. Princess to-laugh.

(23) a. Fokusnik pokazal fokus. Zriteli applodirovat'
Magician (has) performed a trick. Spectators to-applaud.

b. Fokusnik pokazyval fokus. *Zriteli applodirovat'
Magician was performing a trick. Spectators to-applaud.

Corresponding tensed clauses are grammatical both after In-Progress and Culminated events (e.g. in (23b), it is possible to say *carevna smejalas'* 'Princess was laughing", or *carevna načala smejat'sja* 'Princess started to laugh.')

The second prediction is that the Russian RIs must be interpreted as a result of some other event, assumed to be known to other participants in the conversation (that is, by an event already represented in the file.)

This is so because the card representing a RI *is* the Resultant Event card, and has to be interpreted as such. In fact, this is exactly the intuition of how these clauses are understood: as a result, a consequence of some other event. This can be seen clearly from the way the discourse can be paraphrased:

(24) a. Carevna načala xoxotat' potomu čto korol' rasskazal anekdot.
Princess started to laugh because the King has told a joke.
  b. Zriteli načali applodirovat' tak kak fokusnik pokazal fokus.
Spectators started to applaud as the magician has performed a trick.

Any other, "independent", non-resultative interpretation is impossible. In fact, these clauses are impossible without a very specific context that supplies the "projecting" event, that is an event whose culmination resulted in the event described by the RI.

The third characteristic of RIs is that they have an inceptive reading. That is the interpretation of the second clause; in (22a) that is the event of laughing just started; moreover, it started as soon as the first event (king telling a joke) culminated. Incidentally, this is why for some speakers RIs sound better with a temporal deictic marker *tut* which can be translated as 'here', 'then', 'at this moment of narration' (e.g. *tut carevna xoxotat'* 'here Princess to-laugh'.) This is also predicted by the proposed theory. Recall that the first ("projecting") event must be culminated and that the RI's event takes up the projected Event card. Now, according to Pianesi and Varzi 1996 and Giorgi and Pianesi 1997, culminated events are *topologically closed*, which means that their *left and right boundaries* are specified. Moreover, as Giorgi and Pianesi show, the left boundary of Parsons' Resultant eventuality is the right boundary of the culminated event. In terms of the proposed theory, it means that the projected event card has a left boundary temporal specification; that is, that it represents an event that initiates at a particular time t (which is the time of the culmination of the first event.) Hence, the inceptive interpretation of the sentence.

These analyses make several interesting predictions concerning predicates that can and cannot appear in Russian RIs. First, consider

Individual Level predicates (or, in Vendler's 1967 classification *stative* verbs) such as *to be tall, to resemble, to look like,* etc. These predicates are not allowed in the RI constructions:

(25) a. *Tut carevna byt' vysokoj.
  here Princess to-be tall
 b. *Tut carevna napominat' korolevu.
  here Princess to-resemble Queen

The first possible explanation that comes to mind (and that was adopted in Avrutin 1997) is that these predicates do not contribute an event variable (Kratzer 1989), and therefore cannot be represented in the discourse by an Event file card. The sentence thus is uninterpretable since the interpretation through this card is the only available option in the case of RIs.

I believe, however, that this view is not entirely correct. I will have more to say about these predicates in Section 4 when I discuss the English Headlines Register. Let me just point out here that in the model proposed in this chapter, the projected card should be taken as representing an Eventuality -- a notion that comprises both events and states. Thus, strictly speaking, I-level predicates denoting states can still be represented by these cards. Moreover, it can be demonstrated that, contrary to the very strong negative judgements of (25), these sentences can be made somewhat better given that a very specific (pragmatically implausible) context is provided. I will return to this point shortly.

To explain why I-level predicates are (normally) unacceptable in RIs, we need to say something about the discourse representation of clauses containing such predicates. Mussan 1996 points out that (at least some) I-level predicates carry a Life Time Effect. For example, if it is asserted that John is from America, it is presupposed by all participants in the conversation that being from America is a property of John which holds for him since his birth and until his death, and, clearly, during the course of a given conversation. Let us say that, in fact, all I-level predicates carry a presupposition of, at least, the File Time Existence. That is, if *John is tall* is uttered, then it is presupposed that *being tall* has been, and will remain John's property at least for the duration of the entire conversation. And if it is asserted that the Princess resembles the Queen, all participants in the conversation assume that resembling the Queen was, is and will be the property of the Princess at least for the current discourse.

If this hypothesis is correct, we can account for the ungrammaticality of (25) in the following way. An Event(uality) card representing an I-level predicate must have a temporal specification corresponding to the duration of the entire conversation. In other words, such a card cannot represent an eventuality with the left (or right) temporal boundary specified. But this is precisely the case of the projected Event card, which, as I argued above, is to represent the eventuality of the infinitival clause. As this card corresponds to the Resultant event, its left boundary is specified and, therefore, it cannot represent the eventuality of an I-level predicate.

Let me now discuss some marginal cases alluded to above, that is situations when sentences of type (25) become more or less acceptable. As is well known, there is a number of syntactic tests that distinguish Individual and Stage Level predicates. For example, I-level predicates are (normally) impossible in progressive and imperative forms, and they are incompatible with punctual time adverbials:

(26) a. *John is resembling Bill.
　　　b. *John is being tall.
　　　c. *Resemble Bill!
　　　d. *Be tall!
　　　e. *John resembled Bill at 5 p.m.
　　　f. *John was tall at 6 p.m.

At the same time, as often noted in the literature, under some imaginary circumstances, (26) can make sense. For example, if John's height can be changed by giving him some magic pill, which would allow him to voluntarily grow or shrink, it would sound quite natural to say: "Please be tall now!", or "John was tall at 6 p.m., short at 7, and he is now being tall again." Similar examples can be constructed with *resemble*.

What seems to be going on in these cases is that the Discourse Time presupposition is being cancelled. That is to say that the context is constructed in such a way that the property expressed by the predicate does not have to hold for the entire duration of the file (i.e. the conversation.) This means, in turn, that the file cards representing these eventualities are allowed to have temporal specifications shorter than the duration of the file. Thus, (27) is acceptable:

(27) After taking a magic pill, John started to be tall at 5 p.m. and stopped at 7."

Analyses of Russian I-level predicates are analogous. In a world where the Princess has some secret power to actively change her height and appearance, (28) becomes more or less acceptable[39]:

(28) Drakon nabrosilsja na princessu. ???Tut Princessa napominat' lebedja.
Dragon attacked the Princess. Here the Princess to resemble a swan.

Importantly, the interpretation of (28) is that *resembling a swan* just started to be a property of the Princess; in other words, that the left boundary of the eventuality is specified (as the right boundary of another, culminated event.)

3.3. Further Constraints on Russian RIs

The absence of an index on T^0 in these constructions explains two other facts about the distribution of RIs. First, as mentioned above, quantified subjects are not allowed:

(29) a. * Nikto ne xoxotat'
nobody not to-laugh
'Nobody started to laugh'
b. ?* každyj zritel' applodirovat'
every spectator to-applaud
'every spectator started to applaud'
c. * kto xoxotat'?

who to-laugh
'Who started to laugh?'

As T^0 has no index, the subject NP cannot have an index, too. But this is not an option for quantifiers: these elements undergo QR and therefore must bear an index to enter an operator - variable relation. Thus, the "indexless" representation of (29) is uninterpretable and is ruled out.

Notice also that if D-linked QPs do not undergo QR (Pesetsky 1987), they should be allowed in RIs. This is indeed the case: (30) is significantly better than (29).

(30) a. ??Tut každyj zritel' v zale applodirovat'
here every spectator in the theatre to-applaud
'every spectator in this theatre started to applaud'
b. ??kto iz nix xoxotat'?
which of them to-laugh
'Which of them started to laugh?'

Another constraint imposed on RIs is that they are impossible in embedded clauses:

(31) a. *Ivan dumal čto carevna xoxotat'.
Ivan thought that princess to-laugh
b. *Artisty xoteli čtoby zriteli applodirovat'.
Actors wanted that[SUBJ] spectators to-applaud
c. *Ja nadejalsja čto gosti kričat' ot radosti
I hoped that guests to-cry loud out of joy

Neither Indicative (a,c), not Subjunctive (b) embedded clauses allow infinitives. To explain this ungrammaticality, I will assume Gueron and Hoekstra's 1995 Tense Chain theory. According to these authors, e, T^0 and Comp form a chain, and therefore must be coindexed. Since e and T^0 in these constructions are indexless, they cannot form a chain with Comp; thus, the sentences are ruled out.[40]

Finally, let me briefly address one more fact about Russian RIs. Most speakers strongly prefer agentive subjects in these constructions, preferably animate NPs that denote individuals actively involved in the action. Thus, (a) and (b) are better than (c) and (d):

(32)   a. Tut rebenok prygat' ot radosti.
          here child to jump of joy.
       b. Tut sobaki rvat' mjaso na časti.
          here dogs to tear meat into pieces
       c. ??Tut stol padat'
          here table to fall
       d. ??Tut tuča rasti.
          here cloud to grow

The example in (33) is particularly telling as it shows a clear-cut division between speakers who are willing to attribute animate character to a computer, and those who are not. Only the first group seemed to accept this sentence:

(33) Tut kompjuter gudet'/dumat'.
       here computer to buzz/to think

A tentative explanation for this phenomenon relies on the idea that animate, active participants in events are *better accessible individuals* (see Ariel 1990). Recall now that the subject NP in these constructions has no index and therefore cannot be represented in the discourse by an individual file card with a specific number[41]. Rather, it is interpreted as a participant in the event represented by the (projected) event card. Since the interpretation of the subject is indirect, the better accessible NPs (e.g. animate agents) are judged to be more acceptable in Russian RIs. Clearly, in Tensed clauses, where both T^0 and subject NP has an index, and the NP is represented by an individual file card, no such contrast exists:

(34) a. Rebenok prygal.
        child jumped
     b. Sobaki rvali mjaso
        dogs tore meat
     c. Stol padal

table fell
d. Tuča rosla
cloud grew

In contrast to (32), all sentences in (34) are equally acceptable.

Finally, we can ask how the Case requirements are satisfied in Russian root infinitives. Notice that the subject NP in these constructions shows up in their default, non-structural case, which in Russian is Nominative:

(35) a. It's her/*she.
    b. Eto ona/*ee
       it (is) she/*her
    c. Eto   Marija/*Mariju/*Marii
       it (is) Marija[NOM]/*Marija[ACC]/*Marija[DAT]

Both pronouns and names show up in the Nominative case. Thus, it is not surprising that when pronouns occur as subjects of root infinitives in Russian, they show up in their default, Nominative form.

(36) Korol' rasskazal princesse anekdot. Ona/*Ee/*Ej xoxotat'.
    The King told the Princess a joke. She/*Her[ACC]/*Her[DAT] to-laugh.

The Case requirements are satisfied by assigning the subject NP a default lexical case. Let me turn now to another case of root infinitive clauses, this time in English.

4. The Headline Register

In this Section, I provide discourse - based analyses of the so-called Headlinese (Stowell 1996, Schutze 1997, Avrutin 1997), exemplified in (37).

(37) a. PRESIDENT TO VISIT RUSSIA
     b. UNIONS TO GO ON STRIKE
     c. McDONALD'S TO SERVE BEER.

An intuitive view on this type of construction is that in order to save the headline space, editors simply drop "irrelevant" material such as modal *be*. For example, (37a) should read as 'President is to visit Russia', with *is* dropped.

There are various reasons to question this simplified view of headlines. First of all, the "space limitation" argument characterises *conditions* when a certain register is used, but does not provide a linguistic analysis of this construction. Moreover, it is not clear why *to* cannot be dropped as well, after all, the headline will still be interpretable and even more space will be saved. More importantly, there are linguistic constraints that cannot be explained by simply saying that something is dropped to save space. Stowell 1996, for example, shows that the distribution of definite and indefinite NPs in Headlines is subject to specific linguistic constraints, an issue that I will not address here.

In fact, a closer look at headlines shows that their intended meaning is slightly different from a corresponding sentence with a modal *be*. Consider for example (38).

(38) a. CLINTON TO VISIT RUSSIA
b. Clinton is to visit Russia.

If (a) and (b) differed only in the phonological realisation of *is*, that is they are different at PF but identical at LF, we would expect them to have identical interpretations. This is not the case, however. In (38b), the sentence has a modal meaning corresponding to a certain obligation on the part of Clinton, and an implied high probability (but not necessity, see below) that he will fulfil his obligation. (38a), on the other hand, means that a certain event *will* take place. This difference shows up in the contrast between (39a) and (39b).

(39) a. Clinton is to visit Russia. But he won't.
b. CLINTON TO VISIT RUSSIA. * BUT HE WON'T.

Only in (a) can the implication associated with modality be cancelled; in (b) the negation results in anomaly. This contrast shows that the two sentences are not identical in their intended meanings.

Let me turn now to the analyses of Headlines, which, as will be seen shortly, are similar to the Russian RIs. To begin with, I follow Roberts' (1993) analyses who argued that the infinitival particle *to* occupies the head of the Tense projection (T^0). Clearly, *to* does not denote any time interval, thus, as in Russian RIs, English T^0 has no index. Following the discussion in Section (3), the event variable e contributed by the predicate, and the subject NP are indexless, too:

(40) PRESIDENT T^0 TO VISIT(e) RUSSIA

This sentence is syntactically well-formed but uninterpretable. As in the case of Russian RIs, the only way to obtain an interpretable representation is to introduce an Event(uality) file card representing the event of the Headline by some discourse - based, non-syntactic way. Notice that (at least intuitively) this event also describes an eventuality that takes place as a result of some state of affairs discussed in the text under the headline. For example, (41) is an appropriate headline for a text discussing some event resulting in the unions going on strike.

(41) UNIONS TO GO ON STRIKE

The relevant text may cover the deadlocked negotiations between the administration and the unions, or some other state of affairs that resulted in the strike. In other words, as in the case with Russian RIs, the event denoted by the Headline is interpreted as a consequence of some other event specified in the discourse.

There are several differences between Russian RIs and headlines, of course. One of them is the temporal interpretation: unlike Russian sentences, headlines do not speak of an event that initiates immediately after the culmination of the other event. Rather, the interpretation is that this event will take place some time in the future. In terms of Reichenbach 1947, the Event time follows the Speech time, as in (42), while (43) corresponds to the Russian RI:

(42) S,R _____ E

(43) R,E _____ S

S here stands for the Speech time, *E* for the Event time, and *R* for the Reference time. I propose that the difference between the two types of root infinitives is due to the presence of *to* in headlines. Specifically, suppose that *to* contributes a semantic feature [+irrealis], which is interpreted in the temporal domain as [-past] (see Gueron and Hoekstra 1995)[42]. In the discourse, the headline event is represented by a new Event card, which is projected as a Resultant Event file card. But due to the presence of *to*, it is interpreted as temporally "disjoint" from the culminated event, that is as an event whose left boundary is not identical to the right boundary of the culminated event. Therefore, the headlines do not have an inceptive reading characteristic of the Russian RIs.

Notice that some properties of the Russian RIs are predicted also to hold for headlines. For example, since T^0 has no index, it cannot be part of a T^0 chain formed with Comp. The headlines thus should not be possible in embedded contexts, which is a correct prediction:

(44) a. *STATE DEPARTMENT ANNOUNCES THAT CLINTON TO VISIT RUSSIA
   b. *WORKERS HOPE THAT UNIONS TO GO ON STRIKE

As in Russian, quantified subject NPs are judged at best as marginal (although I found some variation among speakers in this case):

(45) a. PRESIDENT TO VISIT RUSSIA. *BUT NOBODY TO MEET WITH YELTSIN.
   b. REPUBLICANS TO LOWER TAXES. *WHO TO PAY THE BILL?

Since quantifiers require an index at LF to enter an operator - variable relation, both T^0 and NP must have indices. Thus, (45) is ruled out, although, as in Russian, D-linked quantifiers are more acceptable:

(46) a. ??WHICH OF THE TWO PARTIES TO PAY THE BILL?
   b. ??NONE OF THE US SENATORS TO VISIT RUSSIA THIS YEAR

Notice that headlines seem to require the "completed" interpretation: it is asserted that the event expressed by the headline will *take place*, not that it will be *taking place*. For example, (40) describes the whole event of visiting Russia by the President, not merely that the visit will begin, or that it will be going on in the future. This can be better illustrated with Accomplishment predicates (see Vendler 1967), such as *draw a circle*. For the sentence *John drew a circle* to be true, it is necessary that the circle be completely drawn by John, not just that he began or is in the process of drawing. Consider now headline (47).

(47) YELTSIN TO DRAW A CIRCLE

The interpretation is that the circle will actually be drawn, not that Yeltsin will begin and will be engaged in the process of drawing a circle. In other words, the event is interpreted as having *a right boundary*.

To explain why English headlines (but not Russian RIs) always have such an interpretation, I will assume featural analyses of English verbs proposed by Giorgi and Pianesi (1997). According to these authors, English verbs always contain in their specification feature [+perfect], in addition to features [+V, -N]. In other languages, such as Italian or Russian, verbs are associated with typical verbal features, such as +V, -N, person and number, but not with the aspectual feature of perfectivity. Giorgi and Pianesi's argument is based on the morphosyntactic "simplicity" of English verbs (e.g. *dress, dream,* etc., which, by themselves, are not even distinguishable from nouns), and on the complexity of Italian verbs, which are always complex words. As Russian is similar to Italian in this sense, I will not further discuss their argument but will assume that Russian verbs do not contain an aspectual feature in their specification, while English verbs do.

Since English verbs are [+perf], the event expressed by an infinitival headline is interpreted as having a specific right boundary. Russian verbs, on the other hand, do not contain a perfective feature, and, therefore, RIs are interpreted as denoting inceptive events with an unspecified right boundary.

As headlines denote events whose left boundaries are not determined (they are "disjoint"), these constructions are compatible with temporal adverbials:

(48) a. YELTSIN TO VISIT CHINA NEXT WEEK
     b. UNIONS TO GO ON STRIKE TOMORROW

This is another difference from the Russian RIs, which do not allow temporal adverbials, as mentioned in Section 3.

Let me turn now to Individual Level predicates in the Headline register. In Avrutin (1997), I claimed that these predicates are always ungrammatical in Headlinese. The analyses were based on Kratzer's 1989 idea that I-level predicates do not contribute an event variable, and therefore cannot be represented through an Event file card.

Colin Phillips, however, pointed out to me that this observation is not entirely correct (e-mail communication, February 1997). I-level predicates seem to be acceptable in headlines, but with a very specific reading, similar to the readings of Russian RIs, as discussed in Section 3. For example, (49) is more or less acceptable assuming that Yeltsin will undergo brain surgery that will change his intellectual capacity:

(49) ?YELSTSIN TO BE INTELLIGENT

(50) ?RUSSIAN PRIME MINISTER TO RESEMBLE PEROT

(50) is acceptable under the assumption that a certain property of the Russian Prime Minster (namely his resembling Perot), which does not hold now, will become true some time in the future, as a result of some event (e.g. cosmetic surgery) discussed in the text under the headline. Such interpretations of I-level predicates are possible in the proposed theory because the file card represents the eventuality without a specific left boundary. Its left temporal boundary is disjoint from the right boundary of the Culminated event. Hence, the interpretation that a certain state of affairs (which does not hold at the moment of speech) will take place in the future. A somewhat degraded judgement of (49) and (50) is probably due to the pragmatically marginal presuppositions.

5. Mad Magazine Register

This register that also allows tenseless verbs in main clauses has been extensively discussed in Akmajan 1984 and Schutze 1997. The following examples are from Hyams (1996):

(51) a. John dance. Never in a million years!
b. My brother marry Mary. Over my dead body!
c. Herman eat bean sprouts. Why?

According to the analyses offered in previous sections, these infinitival clauses are also represented in the discourse by Event(uality) cards. This is so because T^0 is unindexed, and so is the subject NP. Thus, the only possible interpretation of the NP is as a participant in the event described by the predicate. As predicted, these clauses cannot be embedded, exactly as in the case of Russian RIs and Headlines:

(52) a. *Mary says that John dance. Never in a million years!
b. *My mother hopes that my brother marry Mary. Never!
c. *I suspect that Herman eat bean sprouts. But why?.

Only clauses with a T^0 bearing an index can be embedded, as T^0 and C^0 are parts of the Tense chain.

Quantifiers seem to be marginal, too, and judgements improve with D- linked quantifiers. Compare (53) and (54).

(53) a. *What?? No one dance? Impossible!!
b. *Who marry Mary? And why??!!
c. *Everyone run a mile every morning??? Incredible!

(54) a. ??What?? None of you dance? Impossible!!
b. ??Which of them marry Mary? And why??!!
c. ??Each of these two boys run a mile every morning??? Incredible!

Thus, because of the indexless character of T^0 in the Mad Magazine sentences, the two constraints discussed above for the Russian RIs and Headlines also hold for this register.

A clear difference lies in the way these clauses are interpreted. First of all, they clearly do not denote either inceptive, or closed events. Rather, a certain attitude is expressed towards an assertion that some event takes place. In other words, I suggest that in order for, say, (51a) to be interpretable, the event of John dancing has to be presupposed. Then, some attitude can be expressed towards this presupposition, e.g. *strange, impossible*, etc., or it can even be denied as a contradiction to the previously existing knowledge (*Never!!!*).

Let me hypothesise that a presupposed event introduces a new Event file card in the discourse that can represent the event of the Mad Magazine clause.

Notice that the left boundary of the event is not specified in this register, that is there is no requirement that the predicate denotes an event that begins to take place at some time. That is why Individual level predicates are acceptable[43]:

(55) a. John fat? Strange!
  b. Mary look like Jane? I doubt it.

Because of the same reason, temporal adverbials are allowed as well:

(56) a. John dance last night??? Impossible!
  b. Mary leave tomorrow??? Disaster!!!

Thus, as in the case of Russian RIs and headlines, the subject NP is interpreted indirectly, as a participant in a certain event. In the case of Mad Magazine clauses, however, the Event file card is not projected (i.e. it does not correspond to a Resultant state), but is introduced in the discourse through a presupposition[44].

6. Achievement Predicates, Perfective Constructions, and Pronouns in Tenselss Clauses

In this section I discuss some other similarities and differences between the three types of Root Infinitival constructions presented in this chapter: Russian RIs, Headlines, and the Mad Magazine register. I will demonstrate that these constructions pattern together with respect to the distribution of perfective clauses, while different from each other with respect to the distribution of achievement predicates and pronouns. I will show how the theory proposed in this chapter accounts for these similarities and differences.

6.1. Achievement Predicates

Achievement predicates, such as *reach the top, win the race, sign the bill*, pattern differently across the three constructions:

Russian RIs:
(57) a. *Tut al'pinist dostigat' veršinu.
      here (the) mountain climber to reach (the) top
   b. *Tut bokser pobeždat' nokautom
      here (the) boxer to win (by) knock-out
   c. *Tut Yeltsin podpisat' bill
      here Yeltsin to sign (the) bill

Headlines:
(58) a. MARY SMITH TO REACH THE TOP IN TWO DAYS
   b. TYSON TO WIN THE FIGHT
   c. CLINTON TO SIGN THE CRIME BILL

Mad Magazine:
(59) a. What??? Mary reach the top in two days? You are kidding!!!
   b. Tyson win the fight??!! Never!
   c. Clinton sign the bill??!! Impossible...

Thus, achievement predicates are allowed in the Headlinese and Mad Magazine, but are disallowed in the Russian RIs.

To explain these facts, I adopt the generalisation in Giorgi and Pianesi (1997), who, in turn, follow Klein (1992), which is given in (60) (G. and P., p. 135):

(60) A consequent state cannot be definite.

A consequent state is definite whenever both its boundaries are definite. In our terms, an Event File card representing a Resultant state cannot be interpreted as having specific left and right temporal boundaries. Let me show now how this constraint explains the above differences between the three types of infinitival clauses.

First of all, since (60) applies only to consequent (resultant) states, it has nothing to say about the Event file cards that were introduced by some other way (not as a result of projection). Thus, it has nothing to say about the Mad Magazine clauses, whatever predicates they contain. As we see (59) is, indeed, grammatical.

Second, notice that achievement predicates necessarily denote events with a specific right boundary (*topologically closed events*, as in Giorgi and Pianesi 1997.) Moreover, Russian RIs are represented by projected Event cards whose left boundary is determined by the right boundary of the culminated event. In other words, their left boundary is always specified. If the predicate in the RI is an achievement predicate, *both* its left and right boundaries are specified, which means that the event is definite. But this contradicts the constraint in (60), hence the ungrammaticality of the Russian RIs with achievement predicates in (60).

The situation is different with headlines, though. Recall that these events, although represented by projected cards, are disjoint from the corresponding culminated events. This means that, unlike Russian RIs, their left boundary is not specified. Then, even if the predicate in the headline is an achievement predicate, that is if the right boundary of the event is specified, it does not result in the event being definite: only its right, but not its left boundary is specified. As the event is not definite, the sentences are grammatical, as shown in (58). Thus, the proposed theory correctly predicts the differences between the Russian RIs, on the one hand, and Headlines and Mad Magazine sentences, on the other.

6.2. Perfective Constructions

Perfective constructions, on the other hand, are uniformly unacceptable across the three types of tenseless clauses:

(61) *Tut Boris narubit' drova (o.k.: ... *rubit'* ... 'to-chip')
here Boris to-have-chopped firewood
'Boris has chipped firewood'

(62) *CLINTON TO HAVE VISITED RUSSIA BY MAY.

(63) *John/*him/*he have danced? Never!

With regard to the Russian RIs in (61), it will suffice to note that perfective constructions denote events with a definite right boundary. As discussed in the previous section, the left boundary of these events are defined as the right boundary of the culminated event. This means that (61) will denote a definite event, which contradicts the requirement in (60). Thus, in the case of Russian, the explanation is identical to the one with achievement predicates.

The situation is different with (62) and (63), however, since the left boundary of the events in this case is not definite. Even if the right boundary is specified, as in the case with perfective constructions, the sentences should still be acceptable, which is not the case. Notice, however, English perfective constructions require an auxiliary verb. But, according to the Tense Chain theory (Gueron and Hoeskra 1995), adopted in this work, auxiliaries must always be part of the T-chain. It follows that the C^0, AUX, T^0 and e must all be coindexed (thus providing a temporal interpretation of a culminated event), which is not the case in headlines or Mad Magazine clauses. Since the Tense Chain condition is violated, (62) and (63) are ruled out.

6.3 Pronouns in Tenseless Clauses

The distribution of pronouns shows another difference between the three types of infinitival clauses. In this case, Russian RIs pattern together with the Mad Magazine sentences in that both of them, but not headlines, allow subject pronouns:

(64) Carevne rasskazali anekdot. Ona xoxotat'.
Princess was told a joke. She to laugh.

(65) John???!!! Him dance??? Impossible

(66) a. ATTENTION READER! YOU ARE TO WIN $1,000,000!
 b. ATTENTION READER! *YOU TO WIN $1,000,000!
 c. YELTSIN APPOINTS HIS DAUGHTER. SHE IS TO BUILD MARKET ECONOMY
 d. YELTSIN APPOINTS HIS DAUGHTER. *SHE/*HER TO BUILD MARKET ECONOMY
 e. TYSON CLAIMS: "I AM TO WIN!"
 f. TYSON CLAIMS: "*I/*ME TO WIN!"

The explanation I propose is based on the following theory of phrase structure developed in Giorgi and Pianesi (1997). According to these authors, languages may differ in the featural composition of various projections. In English, for example, agreement and tense features belong to the same bundle and therefore project a single category AGR/T:

(67)
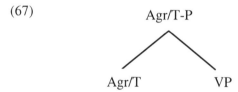

In Italian, and I argue in Russian as well, agreement and tense features belong to different feature bundles and project separate projections AgrSP and TP, as in (68).

(68)
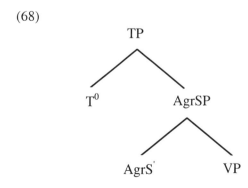

Moreover, I hypothesise that for a pronoun to be *identifiable,* it needs to be *supported* by the presence of agreement feature in a corresponding functional projection. Pronouns, in some sense, are referentially deficient (compared to R-expressions) in that they have to be interpreted with the help of some other elements: operators (when pronouns are interpreted as bound variables), R-expressions (when pronouns are referring), or as deictic elements. Thus, I assume that pronouns can be fully interpretable (identifiable) only if the clause contains a projection with agreement features[45].

Notice now that only headlines require an infinitival particle *to*. Suppose that this particle can appear in AGR/T position only under condition that this projection is completely "empty", that is it contains no features whatsoever. Crucially, it must have no agreement features. The particle *to* in this sense is an overt marker of the featureless nature of a functional head. It follows then that pronouns cannot appear in a headline, which is shown to be true in (66).

In Russian, on the other hand, agreement features project its own projection. I assume that these features in Russian are always present (notice that there is no infinitival particle comparable with *to* in English.) In this case, pronouns should be acceptable in Russian RIs, as demonstrated in (64).

Regarding Mad Magazine sentences, I will simply assume that they are similar to small clauses in that they contain agreement features (though no tense features). It may be the case that the features are *scattered* (as in Giorgi and Pianesi's proposal), with agreement features heading their own projection. Or, there is only one projection AGR/T-P, which contains only agreement features. The choice between the two options is not crucial for my purposes. Importantly, the relevant position is not completely empty, therefore *to* is not allowed:

(69) *John to dance??? Never!!!

But due to the presence of agreement features, pronouns are allowed, as demonstrated in (65)[46,47].

7. The Optional Infinitive Stage

7.1. Presuppositional Introduction of an Event File Card

As mentioned in Section 1 of this Chapter, young children pass through the stage in their linguistic development when they allow untensed verbs in the main clauses. Some relevant examples are repeated below.

(70) a. Michelle dormir   (French: Pierce 1989)
       Michelle sleep
   b. Pappa schoenen wassen   (Dutch: Weverink 1989)
       daddy shoes wash
   c. Thorstn das haben   (German: Wexler 1994)
       Thorsten that have
   d. Mommy eat cookie   (English: Radford 1990)

As we have seen above, Root Infinitives are also allowed in some adult registers, provided that certain discourse conditions are satisfied. In what follows, I will argue that children's RIs do not violate any syntactic conditions on a sentence's well-formedness, but rather represent an abnormal introduction of an Event file card into discourse.

I propose that young children allow a non-syntactic, presuppositional introduction of an Event card. In this sense, the discourse representation of a RI in child speech is similar to the Mad Magazine register, although the range of pragmatic circumstances when this representation is possible is larger than in adult speech. Children can be said to describe a certain situation in terms of *events*, rather than in terms of individuals involved in some action. The meaning of the sentence, its truth condition, remains the same; what differs is the way in which this proposition is represented in the discourse. When expressing a proposition "Mummy is eating a cookie", children represent it in the discourse by presupposing an

Event card (a situation) rather than introducing this card by translating the index of an event variable (and indices on subject and object NPs as numbers of the individual file cards inside the Event card.)

(71)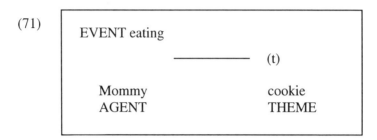

As in the case with adult RIs, T^0 and subject NP have no indices, and the subject NP is interpreted indirectly, as a participant in the event. Unlike the Mad Magazine clauses, however, children allow these sentences without any specific contextual circumstances. On the other hand, RIs in child English are different from Headlines. Recall that in English AgrS and T^0 project one functional category AGR/T-P. My claim is that AGR/T-P has no index as it lacks necessary features contributed (usually) by finite T^0. I further argued that in headlines agreement features are also missing which made, on the one hand, the insertion of *to* possible, and, on the other, the subject pronoun impossible. Suppose now that in children's RIs, agreement features *are* present. The non-finite AGR/T-P still has no index but since *to* is possible only in the absence of any features, this particle should not occur in children's RIs. Indeed, sentences like 'Mommy to eat cookie' are not observed in child speech. Furthermore, since the agreement features are present, the subject pronoun in children's RIs, unlike the headlines, should be allowed. This is indeed the case: pronouns are often observed as subjects of RIs in English speaking children[48].

Let us see now how this proposal accounts for the empirical data observed in child speech. First of all, it is predicted that in those constructions where T^0 must bear an index because of some syntactic constraints, RIs should be impossible. This is so because, as argued throughout this book, children do not violate any syntactic constraints.

Indeed, there is evidence that this prediction is borne out. As discussed above, (following Gueron and Hoekstra 1995) auxiliaries must be part of the Tense chain. Therefore, they must bear an index because all members of the chain must be coindexed. If so, auxiliaries are predicted to be always tensed. In fact, this is precisely what is observed in child speech: Crisma 1992 (among others) shows that children do not allow untensed auxiliaries even at the stage when main verbs appear in their infinitival forms.

Furthermore, the proposed analyses predict that in those cases where T^0 undergoes overt movement, Root Infinitives should be impossible. This is so because the moved T^0 must bind its trace; binding requires coindexation, which means that T^0 must bear an index. The relevant evidence comes from languages that exhibit I^0 to C^0 movement. As shown in Phillips 1995, there are no Root Infinitives in Wh-questions in languages with I^0 to C^0 movement, although RIs in Wh-questions in other languages (e.g. English) are observed (see Roeper and Rohrbacher 1994, Bromberger and Wexler 1995).

The second prediction is that quantifiers should not appear as subjects of RIs in child speech because, as discussed above, these elements always require an index at LF, which means that T^0 must also bear an index. Unfortunately, this prediction is not fully testable because at the age when children allow root infinitives, they hardly use any quantifiers at all, either in tensed, or untensed clauses[49].

The next prediction has to do with the availability of untensed clauses in embedded constructions. As mentioned above, infinitives are disallowed in embedded clauses in all three constructions discussed above. We predict then that they should not be found in embedded clauses in children's speech. This prediction again is not directly testable because by the time when children use longer sentences they are usually out of the Optional Infinitive stage. However, indirectly, this prediction is borne out[50]. Hyams (1996) relates the availability of root infinitives to the availability of null subject in the speech of children acquiring non-pro-drop languages, such as English. According to her analyses, the subject of these constructions for children is PRO. PRO is allowed precisely because Tense is unindexed which makes PRO ungoverned. Moreover, Valian (1991) noticed that English-speaking children do not allow null subjects in embedded clauses. Thus, the fact that PRO is not allowed for English-speaking children in embedded clauses can be used as indirect evidence for the fact that Tense must bear an index in this case, exactly as it does in the case of embedded clauses in adult grammar discussed in the previous sections.

Interestingly, RIs do not appear with all kinds of verbs at the Optional Infinitive stage. For example, Wijnen 1997, in an experimental study demonstrated that Dutch-speaking children use both finite and non-finite forms with eventive verbs (e.g. *bouwen* 'to build'), but only finite forms with non-eventive verbs (e.g. *heeft* 'possesses'). Moreover, sentences with the verb *to be* (e.g. as in (72)) are unattested in child speech, and, as reported in Ingram and Thompson 1996, among others, modals are always tensed.

(72) Mummy be hungry.

With regard to (72) and modals, I will simply follow Wexler (1995) and Hyams (1996) who argue that (probably because of its featural composition) *be* must always bear an index, or, in other words, be tensed. In their analyses, this requirement comes from the constraints on the interpretability.

To explain why children produce significantly more untensed clauses with activity verbs, we need to recall how the subject NP is interpreted in this case. Given that the subject does not bear an index, the corresponding file card does not have a number, and is interpreted indirectly, as a participant in the event represented by the presupposed file card. Recall also that in Section 3 of this chapter, I mentioned that Russian RIs are more acceptable with agentive, animate subject NPs. I speculated that this has to do with the fact that such NPs are more easliy accessible in the discourse. I hypothesise that the same holds for the children's RIs. The subject of an activity verb is usually a more prominent entity (i.e. an animate agent) than the subject of stative verb (e.g. a theme, animate, or inanimate). Thus, subjects of the activity

7.2. Null Subject Languages

Let me turn now to the discussion of RIs in null subject languages, more precisely to the absence of these constructions in the speech of children acquiring null subject languages (for discussion see Rizzi 1994, Wexler 1995, Phillips 1996, Hyams 1996, among others).

Notice, first of all, that (at least some) null subject languages have specific registers that allow RIs in adult grammar. Thus, Rizzi (1994) gives the following examples from Italian[52]:

(73) a. Io fare questo? Mai!
   me to-do that? never!
   b. Partire immediatamante!
   to-leave immediately

Thus, we are faced with the following dilemma: On the one hand, Italian-speaking children do not produce (or produce significantly less) RIs than English-speaking children of the same age. On the other hand, it is not the case, that there is something special about Italian grammar that always and completely disallows RIs: as (73) shows, these constructions are sometimes possible in adult Italian. The explanation, therefore, should be two-fold. First, assuming that there is no fundamental difference between English and Italian children, it has to provide an account of the difference between the English and Italian languages that would show why the RIs are found much more often in English. Second, the theory should explain the relevant difference between Italian children and adults because adults (in some cases) do produce RIs.

My explanation will be based on the assumption that in non-null subject languages (e.g. English) the subject NP is in [Spec, AGR/T-P], while in null subject languages (e.g. Italian), it is in [Spec, AgrSP]. It follows then that in untensed clauses, that is when Tense has no index, the subject NP must be indexless *only in English*, but not in Italian. In

Italian, AgrS always has the necessary features, and, in terms of the proposed model, always bears an index. In this case, the subject NP must also have an index, which makes Italian RIs different from the English ones.

(74)
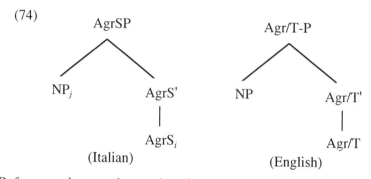
(Italian)   (English)

Before turning to the explanation of the observed cross-linguistic variation, let me introduce some notation. First, I assume that the linguistic operations discussed throughout this book have "psycholinguistic relevance", in the sense that they require a certain amount of processing resources for their implementation. The amount may differ, of course, depending on the nature of the operation. Thus, let **R(e)** be the amount of resources necessary for the introduction of an Event file through presupposition (as in the case of children's RIs). Let **R(i)** be the amount of resources necessary for instantiating the variable index on an NP with a number of an individual file card. Obviously, there are other operations that require resources, such as phonological, morphological, syntactic (e.g. phrase-building), etc. But I will abstract away from these operations because, as we will see, the proposed explanation will rely on the relationship between R(e) and R(i).

Suppose now that an English-speaking child wants to express a proposition that his/her mother is running. The child can either produce a full tensed clause ('Mommy runs'), or produce a RI ('Mommy run'). If the clause is tensed, both the subject NP, AGR/T-P and the event variable e have indices. Their instantiation (i.e. the syntax - discourse interface) will require the following amount of resources:

(75) $R_{tensed} = R_{NP}(i) + R_T(i) + R_e(i)$

To produce a RI, on the other hand, the child must allocate $R_{untensed} = R(e)$, that is resources necessary for the introduction of the Event file card. Suppose now that $R(e) < R_{NP}(i) + R_T(i) + R_e(i)$. Assuming that the child's processing resources are limited, the child may choose (at least in some cases, and at least some children) a less expensive option, that is, to introduce an Event file card through presupposition, not by syntactic means. Notice that the child does not violate any syntactic constraints: RIs are well-formed constructions and they do appear in the adult speech as well. This approach would also explain why there is a certain variation in the number of RIs between English-speaking children: it is natural that the amount of resources may vary from child to child.

Consider now an Italian-speaking child. This child can also produce a tensed clause with the amount of resources equal to $R_{tensed} = R_{NP}(i) + R_T(i) + R_e(i)$. Or, he/she can opt for a RI. The difference between English and Italian, however, is that $R(e)$ is not *all* that is needed in this case in Italian. Since subject NP in this language is in [Spec, AGR/T-P], and therefore always has an index, even if the child presupposes an Event file card, the index on the subject NP must be instantiated. This requires additional resources: $R_{NP}(i)$. Thus, the RIs in Italian are more 'expensive' than in English:

(76) a. $R_{untensed} = R(e) + R_{NP}(i)$ (Italian)

b. $R_{untensed} = R(e)$ (English)

Suppose now that ($R_{untensed} = R(e) + R_{NP}(i)) > (R_{tensed} = R_{NP}(i) + R_T(i) + R_e(i))$. If this is so, the Italian-speaking child will produce significantly more tensed clauses that untensed (because it is "cheaper"), and significantly more tensed clauses than an English-speaking child.

Notice also that this approach explains why RIs exist in some adult Italian registers. Unlike children, adult speakers produce RIs because of some discourse-related, contextual circumstances, *not* because of processing constraints. In Italian, we just saw, these constructions are "more expensive" than tensed clauses, but since, presumably, normal adult speakers have enough resources, they can produce these constructions when they are required. Children, on the other hand, do not produce them, *precisely* because their resources are limited and they opt for a "cheaper" way of expressing a thought. It so happens, that, because of the structural differences between languages, the cheapest way in English is a RI, while in Italian it is a tensed clause[53].

8. Root Infinitives in the speech of Broca's aphasics

It is interesting and important for the proposed "processing" account of the Optional Infinitive stage that agrammatic Broca's aphasics demonstrate similar performance. Some examples, reported by Gleason et al 1975, are given in (77).

(77) a. Dog chase cat
b. The baby cry

The same data are reported in a number of other languages. Thus, commenting on the existence of infinitives in agrammatic German speech, Goodglass and Geschwind 1976 write: "...since the German infinitive, unlike the English, has an inflectional ending, this evidence supports the view that the agrammatic ... is not merely dropping the person and tense marker in English..." (see also Nespoulos et al. 1990, Lesser and Milroy 1993). For a comprehensive review and cross-linguistic examples of aphasic speech the reader is referred to Menn and Obler (1990).

This similarity between children and Broca's aphasics should not be surprising. As I argued in previous chapters, in a number of constructions that require additional processing resources, these patients demonstrate a poor performance, compatible with the performance demonstrated by children. This was the case with the distinction between referential and bound variable pronouns, the comprehension of contrastive stress by these two populations, priming for the most frequent meaning of an ambiguous word, and other results.

Moreover, if the aphasic errors are related to the lack of processing resources, we can expect that, like children, these speakers will not violate any syntactic constraints. Indeed, Herman Kolk (personal communication, November, 1998) has informed me that Dutch-speaking aphasics almost never use RIs with modal and auxiliary verbs, although the use of RIs in Dutch-speaking Broca's aphasics (and children) is a well-documented fact (see, for example, Kolk and Heeschen 1990, 1992, Bastiaanse 1995, de Roo, 1998. Bastiaanse and Jonkers (1998) also report that copula verbs and modals in the speech of agrammatic aphasics are always tensed. Recall that modal verbs and auxiliaries must be part of the Tense Chain, and, therefore, the tense node in clauses containing these elements must bear an index. As predicted, both children (see discussion above) and Broca's aphasics correctly produced tensed forms of these elements.

Further similarities between children and aphasics can be found in the correlation between the finiteness of the verb and its structural position. German-speaking children, for example, almost always correctly move the verb into a second position (as it should be in adult German) when the verb is tensed while leaving it at the sentence-final position when the verb is infinitival. (see Poeppel and Wexler (1993) and reference cited therein). Pierce (1992) showed that French-speaking children use non-finite verbs only after the negation *pas*, while moving it to the position in front of *pas* when the verb is tensed. These authors argue that at a very early age children know the necessary *syntactic* constraints on the distribution of tensed verbs and that they possess – very early – the knowledge of verb movement in their languages.

Interestingly, exactly the same correlation was reported for Dutch- and German-speaking aphasics. Kolk and Heeschen (1992) found that if a non-finite verb is produced by an aphasic speaker, this verb, in the vast majority of cases (over 90%), is in the clause final position.

The theory outlined in this chapter makes further predictions regarding the use of non-finite verbs by Broca's aphasics. Recall that, as in the case of various normal adult registers, RIs are impossible in embedded clauses. This is so because the embedded tense must be coindexed with Comp in order to satisfy the tense chain condition. While such constructions are not directly testable with children (because they don't produce, at the relevant age, embedded clauses), they can be tested with aphasic speakers. There are clear predictions in this case: these subjects should use non-finite verbs only in main clauses, but not in embedded contexts.

In fact, these are exactly the results of a recent study by Bastiaanse and van Zonneveld (1998). Ten agrammatic Broca's aphasics (all native speakers of Dutch) were asked to complete a sentence with a missing verb. In one condition, the verb was to be inserted into a main clause (as in (78)), and in the other condition it was in the embedded clause, as in (79).

(78) de boer ... de koe
 the farmer ... the cow
 'The farmer milks the cow.'
(79) ik zie dat de man het koor ...
 I see that the man the choir ...
 'I see that the man directs the choir.'

Overall, subjects produced finite verbs in the main clause in 49% of the cases, thus demonstrating a performance very similar to the children's Optional Infinitive stage. In the embedded clauses, however, they correctly produced finite verbs in 86% of the cases, thus showing a significantly better performance. These results are especially interesting because the embedded clauses are longer and, thus, could be expected to present more problems for these speakers. This was not the case, however, which demonstrated once again that this population is sensitive to the syntactic constraints.

Finally, the proposed theory makes a prediction regarding aphasic speakers of null subject languages. As in the case with children, these patients should not use Root Infinitives (or they should do it significantly less often than aphasic patients speaking non-null subject languages do.) In fact, this appears to be the case. An informal analysis of the speech of Polish and Italian aphasics, reported in Jarema and Kadzielawa 1990 and Miceli and Mazzuchi 1990, shows a striking difference between the overwhelming use of RIs by, for example, Dutch and German aphasics and a relatively rare production of these forms by Polish and Italian patients. For example, the Italian-speaking aphasics whose data are reported in and Miceli and Mazzuchi 1990 produced (incorrectly) only 4 infinitival verbs out of 27 verb inflection errors. Polish-speaking aphasics appear to make this error even less frequently[54]. This finding is, of course, in sharp contrast to the use of RIs by Dutch, German and English aphasics for whom such an error appears to be a truly characteristic feature of their speech.

Another prediction with regard to the use of RIs by aphasic patients has to do with their use of quantifiers in tensed and untensed clauses. According to the theory outlined above, these patients should produce RIs in sentences with quantified subjects. At the moment, however, I do not have sufficient data to evaluate this prediction, partially because quantifiers are not widespread in the speech of these patients. To find out whether this prediction is borne out or not, a specific experimental procedure has to be carried out. I will leave this for future research.

The comparison of children and aphasics with regard to their use of RIs is very instructive for finding the location and explanation for the observed errors. In the case of children, I suggested that they introduce an Event File Card, which is used to represent the event described by the RI. As in the case with pronouns, it is possible that this error is a result of the lack of knowledge of particular discourse conditions that specify when such use is legitimate. But, in my view, it is implausible that as a result of brain damage, Broca's aphasics lose exactly the same piece of knowledge that is missing in children. Given other similarities between the two populations, and given that their resources are limited, it appears to be more plausible to find an explanation along the lines of this kind of limitation. Both populations in this case will resolve (at least in some occasions), to the use of structures that are well formed syntactically and, at the same time, are more economical, As I suggested above, non-finite matrix clauses appear to be such structures, at least in some languages.

CHAPTER IX

SUMMARY AND CONCLUDING REMARKS

1. The Limitation of Processing Resources as an Explanation of Linguistic Performance

In this book I have discussed various experimental and theoretical studies that addressed the interplay between syntactic and discourse-related knowledge. I have attempted to account for the abnormal performance (comprehension or production) in terms of the limitation of processing resources necessary for the implementation of particular linguistic knowledge. In this sense, the approach I take assumes that the null hypothesis in the study of language acquisition is that children's knowledge is no different from that of normal adults. While this view, of course, is by no means new, a precise picture of what is missing in children, if not knowledge, has been, and probably remains, somewhat vague. Researchers often mention complexity as a factor in children's performance, but equally often this notion does not provide sufficient explanatory power. For example, sentences with quantifiers may appear more complex, in some sense, than sentences with R-expressions; yet the former yield a better performance in children's interpretation of pronominals.

The approach adopted in this book is that the relevant notion of complexity is related to the non-syntactic domain. In Chapter II, I have shown that the correct interpretation of NPs requires an integration of syntactic and discourse-related knowledge, and that the crucial difference between the two domains lies in the differences between "speaker-internal" and "conversation-internal" types of knowledge.

SUMMARY AND CONCLUSIONS 177

Various psycholinguistic studies with normal adults mentioned throughout the book showed that the non-syntactic, discourse-related operations require additional resources. It is not surprising then that children's errors appear to reflect this increase in the processing demands.

The limitation of resources may show up in a variety of tasks. In Chapter III, I presented analyses of children's errors with the interpretation of pronominals. In contrast to their good performance with reflexives and pronouns bound by quantified NPs, children demonstrate a chance performance in apparently "simple" Principle B cases. However, in terms of the distinction between syntactic and discourse domains, the notion of "simplicity" turns out to be just the opposite: constructions that require only syntactic knowledge are "simpler" than those that rely on the integration of the syntactic and discourse domains.

In Chapter IV, I presented evidence from various experimental studies that support the main claim of the book. The two discourse-related operations, incorporation and accommodation, are carried out by normal adults differently, the latter being more complex. While this complexity does not cause a breakdown in the adult performance, children's limited resources turn out to be insufficient for the correct implementation of this operation.

Children also demonstrate an abnormal use of definite NPs and deictic expressions in spontaneous speech, picture description tasks and other experimental situations. Overall, it appears that their difficulties are related to figuring out particular discourse conditions when a definite NP can, or cannot be used. This operation requires accessing other speakers' representation of the discourse because, as shown in Chapter II, changes in the speaker's discourse representation are allowed only if other participants in the conversation make analogous changes. The claim thus is that making inferences about other speakers is sometimes (although not always) beyond children's capacity.

Chapters V and VI discuss children's performance on tasks involving other kinds of pronominals: possessive pronouns in Russian and plural pronouns in English. The analyses offered there support the claim that children differentiate between purely syntactic operations (e.g. an operator – variable relation) and discourse – related operations (e.g. identifying a discourse reference). Even though the constructions involved in these tasks are quite different from each other and from the "simple" Principle B cases discussed in Chapter III, the overall results are consistent with the proposed distinction between the two kinds of linguistic knowledge. The consistency of the results across different languages, different tasks and different types of pronouns can be taken as evidence of the universal nature of the proposed deficit.

While most studies in child language acquisition investigated the interpretation of pronouns as elements that can be interpreted either syntactically or through discourse, recent developments in the linguistic theory suggest that a similar distinction can be made with regard to reflexives. In Chapter VII, I present results of an experimental study based on the Reflexivity theory. The main point here is that only reflexives that are co-arguments with their antecedents are interpreted syntactically, while other reflexives receive a logophoric, discourse-related interpretation. Consistent with other findings, children show a different performance in these two cases demonstrating a significantly better ability to implement the relevant syntactic knowledge.

The discussion in Chapter VIII focuses on an apparently different type of error observed in child speech, the so-called Optional Infinitive stage. The main point of this chapter was to show that children possess a very subtle linguistic knowledge at a very early age, and that their errors are non-syntactic in nature. I have presented analyses of the root infinitive clauses in Russian and English in order to demonstrate that adult speakers do, in fact, allow these constructions, although under very specific contextual circumstances. Thus, in spite of the apparently different nature of the observed errors, the deficit is argued to be also related to the integration of syntactic and discourse – related knowledge.

If children's difficulties with discourse – related constructions are indeed due to the lack of processing resources, no learnability problem arises. Children in fact already possess the relevant knowledge, and they will demonstrate an adult-like performance when their processing capacity fully matures. In this respect it is instructive to compare children's performance with the linguistic performance of other populations whose processing capacity has also been argued to be limited. This is the reason why at various places throughout the book I mentioned some interesting similarities between normally developing children and agrammatic Broca's aphasics. The comparison is not accidental and probably deserves certain clarification.

2. Child Language and Aphasia

The similarities (at least superficial) between the linguistic performance of the two populations did not elude researchers (for more discussion see Caramazza and Zurif 1978 and references cited therein.) The observations of similar speech patterns have given rise to several influential psycholinguistic theories, such as *Ribot's Law*. According to this view (expressed as early as 1883, see Ribot 1883), the order of language development is mirrored, in reverse, by the order of language loss. Put simply, the later a piece of linguistic knowledge is acquired, the more susceptible it will be to be lost in language impairment. In phonology, for example, a particular sound pattern that appears late in child speech is predicted to be more likely to be problematic for brain-damaged patients (aphasics) than a sound pattern present in the speech of younger children. In syntax, structures more problematic for production and comprehension of older children should be missing from the speech of and difficult to comprehend by Broca's aphasics, rather than structures present in the speech of and comprehensible by younger children.

A somewhat similar, but more linguistically based approach is due to Roman Jakobson (e.g. Jakobson 1941), which is known as the Regression Hypothesis. The claim here is that the order of language dissolution is identical to, but yet opposite in direction to the order of language development. In phonology, for example, if the child acquires certain phonological distinctions (e.g. [+labial]/[-labial]) prior to other featural distinctions (e.g. [+voiced]/[-voiced]), it means that the order of dissolution of the linguistic system should be reversed: Aphasic patients should be more likely to first lose the [+/- voiced] distinction, while preserving (at this stage) the [+/- labial] distinction.

A more recent approach to the comparison between the two populations is due to Yosef Grodzinsky (Grodzinsky 1990) and is based on the influential Subset Principle (e.g. Dell 1981, Berwick 1985, Wexler and Manzini 1987). According to this theory, each stage in language development can be characterized by a particular grammar -- a system that can generate all grammatical and no ungrammatical (at this stage) sentences. The linguistic system moves from one grammar to another as a result of changing parameter settings; moreover the development proceeds in such a way that the grammar that generates fewer possible structures ("a more restrictive grammar") necessarily precedes a "more permissible grammar" that can generate more acceptable structures. With regard to language loss, Grodzinsky presents a formal model of the "reverse" development, that is the formal picture of what stages of linguistic dissolution should look like if the language loss, indeed, is identical to, yet opposite in direction to the order of acquisition.

The following three observations are characteristic of the above views. First, no particular reason is given for the existence of the predicted reversal. In other words, there is no independent motivation for the claim that the later a piece of knowledge is acquired the more vulnerable it should be in language impairment. Nor is it clear why the hierarchy of, say, phonological feature acquisition should be reversed in aphasia, or why the parameters should be "re-set" in language breakdown in the order exactly opposite to the way they are set in language development. As these views are formulated, they are more descriptive generalisations (observed and/or predicted) than theoretical systems based on independent motivations.

Second, none of the above approaches make any connections to the psycholinguistic research with normal adult speakers. It is well-

SUMMARY AND CONCLUSIONS

known, however, that even for normal speakers certain linguistic constructions may present more difficulties in processing than the others. It would be fruitful, therefore, to establish whether there is any correlation between the comprehension pattern exhibited by normal adults, on the one hand, and children and aphasics, on the other. Indeed, if it turns out that those constructions that are more complicated for normal adults are also most vulnerable for children and aphasics, such an observation would be more consistent with the view that the actual reason for the errors observed in studies with these two populations have nothing to do with their knowledge of language but rather with their limited ability to implement this knowledge.

Finally, and related to the previous comment, it is important to remember that, as in any other science, psycholinguists deal with empirical observations, and then, based on these observations, attempt to provide theoretical explanations for the collected data. But observations, that is experimental results, can be due to various factors. Linguistic errors in comprehension, for example, can be due to the lack of specific linguistic knowledge required for the correct interpretation of a given sentence, or they can be due to the inability to implement the knowledge, which, by itself, is intact. All of the above approaches, however, unanimously vote to attribute the observed linguistic anomaly to the anomaly of the language faculty (that is to say that the knowledge of language is different from that of normal adult speakers in a particular way -- either because of a hierarchical reversal, or because of a different parameter setting.) While this view, of course, is legitimate, it is by no means the only possible one. Children and aphasics can demonstrate similar problems with some linguistic constructions in spite of the fact that their knowledge of language is no different from that of normal adults. If it were possible to provide independent evidence that certain constructions require more processing resources (and to explain why it should be so), the observed similarities would have a different explanation.

A simple example may illustrate this point. Suppose we observe that my digital watch is showing the wrong time (we have independent evidence of what the correct time is.) In fact, suppose we know that there is a certain area inside this watch such that, when it is damaged, the watch will slow down. We know this by observing many watches with damage to this particular area. We might conclude that some chip, responsible for conducting time measuring operations, is broken, or even missing.

But is this conclusion necessarily correct? Not really. The putative area may contain a battery which, when damaged, will not be able to supply the *intact* mechanism with the necessary amount of power. The result, and our observations, will be the same: the watch is not showing the time shown by other, unimpaired watches. But our conclusions with regard to the function of the damaged area will be wrong.

Children and Broca's aphasics exhibit certain similarities in the pattern of their production and comprehension errors, for example in the interpretation of pronouns, use of definite determiners, root infinitives, lexical access, etc. Rather than explaining these apparently unrelated findings in syntactic terms, I have attempted to account for the observed errors in terms of the lack of processing resources, or energy, necessary for carrying out certain linguistic operations. From an independent linguistic perspective, certain constructions require additional, discourse-related operations. From the processing point of view the observed similarities are not surprising if we make one (rather obvious) assumption: the processing resources in children and Broca's aphasics are limited. In children, because their brains are not yet fully mature, and in aphasics because their brains are damaged[55].

Clearly, more research needs to be done both in aphasiology, language acquisition and neurological development to arrive at a coherent theory of the similarities between children and aphasics. Needless to say, such research must be theory-based: the hypothesis and explanations must be formulated in terms of linguistic theories. Only in this case will the obtained results have descriptive and explanatory power, which is a prerequisite for any scientific theory. But one claim, it seems, can be made now. While it is often tempting to come up with a theory of language acquisition or language impairment formulated in purely structural, formal terms, such a formulation may not always reflect the actual state of affairs. Elegant

SUMMARY AND CONCLUSIONS

and formal in their formulations, linguistic theories are about the human *knowledge of language*. But speakers must have resources to *implement* this knowledge. The correct explanation of observed errors in children and aphasics, thus, may turn out to be less elegant and formal than one might desire.

[1]Somewhat similar examples can be constructed with logophoric reflexives, which will be discussed in Chapter VII.
[2]Examples (5) - (7) are also from Heim 1993.
[3]See also Higginbotham 1985, Reinhart 1983 and Montalbetti and Wexler 1988 for similar proposals.
[4]In fact, this is a simplification of Reinhart's proposal. As discussed in Chapter I, R-expressions can also function as generalized quantifiers. In this case, this expression and the pronoun do receive indices. Thus, in Reinhart's system, assignment of indices is an optional procedure that takes place at LF depending on the interpretation of the NP. My approach is different in that I argue that NPs always bear indices, but their interpretation may be different. See discussion below.
[5]The idea of using indices to express both types of relations is originally due to Heim (1993). Heim's proposal is different from mine in that she argues for the presence of two indices on each NP. The first index (by stipulation) comes from the lexicon, and the second is (optionally) assigned at LF in those cases where NP undergoes QR. The first ("inner") index in this system corresponds to what the NP can be bound by, and the second ("outer") index corresponds to what it can bind. This, rather complicated mechanism, is introduced in order to account for some non-trivial cases of VP-ellipsis.
[6]Other nominal elements that may come from the lexicon with an index are functional categories AgrS and AgrO, which I do not discuss here. Intuitively, the set denoted by Agr is fully determined by its features. If Agr is +sing, +masculine, it denotes the set of all possible singular masculine individuals. An interesting question (which I leave open at the moment) is in what respect (if in any) Agr is different from pronouns, in particular a non-pronominal Agr.
[7]See, for example, Hawkins 1978 and Ariel 1990 for extensive discussions and references.
[8]For more examples of triggering see Hawkins 1978, E. Clark 1977.
[9]I call this card Visual Situation for simplicity only: clearly, as in the case of blind speakers, the situation does not have to be perceived visually. Importantly, though, the objects referred to in a given conversation have to be perceptually accessible to all participants in the conversation.
[10]This is, of course, a very rough description of what an inference might look like. The question of how inferential mechanism works is complicated and depends to a large extent on the question of knowledge representation. For

example, if we assume that various concepts are represented as collections of features, inferences could be said to be based on finding features common for two representations. If we assume that the notion of a concept becomes meaningful only if it is embedded into a theory, inferences will be based on some causal relations between concepts within a particular theory. Some current work in Artificial Intelligence attempts to provide computational analyses of inference (see, for example, Jantke (1986), Winston (1991), and references cited therein).

[11] In languages with overt morphological markers for definite and indefinite NPs, such as English, the use of these markers signals other participants in the conversation of the changes introduced in the speaker's file (e.g. a new card, or incorporation). I assume that it is part of the knowledge of the meaning of the determiner system that all speakers are able to understand this signal. An interesting question is how speakers of languages with no overt determiner system (e.g. Russian) convey to other participants in a conversation the relevant information regarding changes in their files (possible mechanisms are word order and intonation pattern.) But this of course is part of a much bigger issue – the relationship between overt morphological markers and discourse function in general, an issue that I will not address here.

[12] This, of course, does not imply that a sentence 'John saw him' is well-formed when accompanied by the speaker's pointing to John. Clearly, this is not the case. At the same time, the sentence may become more or less acceptable when the pronoun is heavily stressed, especially in the first person: 'I hate ME.' Recall, however, that the use of reflexives in such sentences (e.g. 'John saw himself') does not require an introduction of a new file card, and therefore is to be preferred. It appears that a simple pointing is unable to override the constraint on minimising the size of the file (see Chapter II), while the contrastive stress, in some cases, can do it. Given that speakers know that pointing by itself is not sufficient to override the discourse rules, they will not produce 'John saw him' (pointing to John) because, for the listener, pointing in this case is not a sufficient reason to introduce a new file card.

[13] Note that the fact that children reject (9) shows that it is not just a tendency to say "YES" that makes (4) often good for them. Sentences are good for children if the computations they carry out allow these sentences. In other words, children behave *rationally*: their behavior corresponds to their

computations. For a recent discussion of this issue see Crain and Wexler (1994), Crain and Thornton (1998).

[14] There are a couple of differences between the production results reported in Bloom et al and comprehension results. First, in production, Bloom et al analyze only the first person pronouns, while experiments were carried out with third person pronouns. Second, even in comprehension experiments it is not the case that all children make errors with pronouns. Thus, it is important to compare production and comprehension of individual children, but this, of course, is impossible in the case of database analyses reported in Bloom et al.

[15] When this manuscript was already in press, my attention was drawn to the work of Baauw, Coopmans and Philip (1998). Their research focused precisely on children's interpretation of various clitics in Romance languages. As far as I can see, their results do not contradict the theory proposed in this book. For more discussion, the reader is referred to the original work of these authors.

[16] Crain and McKee use these data to argue against the view proposed by Tavokalian (1978) and Solan (1983) that children first hypothesize a purely linear prohibition against backwards anaphora. Crain and McKee argue that children are sensitive to the structural restrictions, for example locality and c-command.

[17] A typical story goes like this: "Here is Father Bear, here is Rabbit", etc.

[18] Recall that the context may provide some information that would allow such a file to represent one individual under two different guises. No such context is available here. Moreover, proper names (in English, at least) cannot be used deictically (this is probably related to the fact that proper names in English cannot be used with determiners: in some German dialects, where names can be used with determiners, their deictic use appears to be possible, too).

[19] The question arises why children cannot 'go back' and introduce a new card for the pronoun, that is to interpret it deictically. I assume that once a pronoun is incorporated, it no longer exists as a discourse entity and, therefore, there is nothing 'to go back' to. Or, it is possible that it is too expensive to "re-do" the incorporation followed by accommodation involved in the deictic use. In any case, this assumption is supported by experimental results with sentences of type (i).

(i) I know who washed him. Father Bear.

Thornton (1990) reports that children's performance in this case is almost no different form adults'. Notice that this construction is similar to Principle C constructions in that the pronoun here also precedes the R-expression. Since *who* and *him* cannot be coindexed, and since *Father Bear* is coindexed with *who*, it follows that *Father Bear* and *him* are not coindexed. And, as in Principle C constructions, the only grammatical interpretation of this sentence is such that Father Bear washes another Father Bear, which is not the case. Children also correctly reject (i).

[20] A somewhat marginal difference between pronouns and nominals here can be explained if we assume that the introduced card actually facilitates the access to the referent.

[21] Interestingly, French children used *il* even to refer to the balloon without establishing reference (*ballon* is masculine in French).

[22] For more discussion of the development of the non-linguistic system of deixis in children see, for example, Wales 1986, Weissenborn and Klein 1982.

[23] Also these results are. at best, suggestive with respect to the limitations on processing resources, I wanted to mention them here because they represent one of few experiments carried out both with children and aphasics. A more detailed theory of the underlying mechanism of priming and inferencing is needed to make more specific claims, in particular that the mechanism involved in the recognition of a probe is essentially the same as the mechanism involved in allowing the use of a definite NP (say, *the bride*) after another NP (e.g. *a wedding*).

[24] Children's performance on sentences with *kazdyj* 'every' was no different from chance (41% acceptance), that is no different from sentences with a definite NP antecedent. This difference between English and Russian experiments is predicted given the difference between the character of *kazdyj* and *every*. As discussed at some length in Avrutin and Wexler 1992, *kazdyj* can be interpreted sometimes as a D-linked element, which results in its non-quantificational interpretation. In this case, children's performance on this condition is not expected to be different from the R-expression antecedent condition. See Avrutin and Wexler 1992 for more details.

[25] This chapter is a slightly modified version of a squib (co-authored with Rozalind Thornton) that first appeared in Linguistic Inquiry. Reprinted with permission of MIT Press.

[26] HLM note five ways in which a pronoun may be anaphorically related to a plural NP antecedent. Just two of these are considered here.

[27] This set is conceptualized as an object to which it is possible to refer, or to point.

[28] Miyamoto and Crain (1991) found that 3-4-year-olds have a strong preference for the distributive reading (e.g. they allow (11b), but not (11a)). In our study, a somewhat different pattern emerged as we will see below. We attribute the difference to age, since the children in our study were older (4-5 years old).

[29] The experiment also included catch-trials to guard against a bias by children to say "Yes" (and to indicate when such a bias was present).

[30] It is possible that these children have the adult grammar. It is also possible that they lack the collective reading of plural NPs. We did not pursue these alternative possibilities.

[31] An interesting question is why children who only have the collective reading accept the distributive stories. The reason, I believe, is that in principle it is always possible to "collectivise" a distributed set of individuals, that is to represent them as a single conceptual entity. If these children's grammar does not allow for a distributive operator, they have to choose this option. The deficiency of grammar, in this case, will force them to ignore the strongly distributive contextual bias.

[32] The project reported here was carried out in collaboration with Jennifer Cunningham (see Avrutin and Cunningham 1997)

[33] In fact, the situation is more complex here because the antecedent for a non-clause-bounded reflexive must be both logophoric (e.g. the SOURCE) and a grammatical subject. I abstract away here from the syntactic requirement on subjecthood and provide examples (9) and (10) just to illustrate the relevance of the notion of the SOURCE.

[34] I would like to thank Colin Phillips for extensive discussion and criticism of an earlier version of the theory of RIs presented in Avrutin 1997. Thanks to his comments and interesting examples, I significantly revised my analyses, which, I hope, has resulted in a more coherent theory.

[35] As Hyams herself acknowledges, children who make errors with pronouns are significantly older than children who allow root infinitives: "I am going to leave to the side the very reasonable question of why the pragmatics of root infinitives are resolved by about age 3, that is, children give up non-modal root infinitives by about 3, while the principle blocking local coreference between a pronoun and NP antecedent is not apparent for many more years. ... I have nothing to say about this at this point." (p. 19). As we will see below,

this difference is not surprising: I will argue that although both errors with pronouns and Tense are related to the syntax - discourse interface, they represent two distinct kinds of errors.

[36] The time interval can be either open, or closed, that is the event can have either left, or right boundaries. It can also have either both boundaries (topologically closed event), or none (open). I will return to this point later.

[37] In Avrutin 1997, I suggested that subject NP is coindexed with T^0, and therefore, with the event variable. The interpretation of such coindexation would be that a given NP is a participant in the event. This does not seem to be correct, however, since both subject and object must be interpreted as participants in the same event. It means that they must bear the same indices, which is clearly false as these NPs do not denote identical individuals.

[38] The index on the object NP means that the object has a referential potential; thus assuming that at LF the object moves to the Spec of AgrO, AgrO will be required to have an index, too. Here, I will focus only on the relation between an NP and T^0.

[39] Many native speakers still judge (28) as extremely marginal, but I think there is an improvement compared to the default context. I speculate that there is a significant variation among speakers w.r.t. their willingness to cancel discourse presuppositions. Another factor that contributes to negative judgements is that Russian RIs are strongly preferred with agentive subjects (I will return to this point shortly). Thus, a highly implausible pragmatic context and the non-agentive character of the subject make (28) significantly less acceptable.

[40] Another possible explanation may be related to the relationship between the matrix and embedded events. Suppose that the matrix verb denotes the anchoring event (Enç 1987, Giorgi and Pianesi 1997), that is that the embedded event must be interpreted (temporally) relative to the matrix event. This, however, contradicts the requirement that the event of the infinitival clause be represented through a projected file card representing a Resultant eventuality of some culminated event. I will not pursue this line of reasoning, however.

[41] The absence of an index on an NP basically means that this NP is "deficient" in some relevant sense: specifically, that it cannot introduce its own, independent file card. In fact, the indexless nature of subject NPs in RIs points to a new line of research, which is far beyond the scope of this book.

Namely, reflexives and pronouns in RIs obey regular Binding Principles, that is the reflexive must be bound, and the pronoun must be free:
President To Hate Himself
*President To Hate Him
John hit himself? Never!!!
*John hit him? Never!!!
Tzarevna bit' sebja po golove.
Princess to-kick herself on the head
Tzarevna bit' ee po golove.
Princess to-kick her on the head
If Binding Principles are formulated in terms of indexation, pronouns and reflexives should be equally possible (or impossible) in these constructions because the subject NP is indexless and, therefore, cannot bind the object. A possible solution may be that NPs, normally, have two indices: one responsible for the lexicon-syntax interface, and the other used for the syntax-discourse interface (the idea of double indexation is not new, see, for example, Fiengo and May 1993, Heim 1993). Intuitively, the double indexing system may be related to the availability of two different types of features (D and N features). This, of course, requires further, extensive investigation.

[42] I assume that Past and Present tenses are [+past].

[43] In Avrutin 1997, I suggested that I-level predicates should not be compatible with this register. However, there seem to be a sufficient number of counterexamples. I thank Ray Jackenodorff, David Pesetsky and Carson Schutze for bringing this matter to my attention.

[44] There are two other constraints in this register that I will not discuss. First, copula *be* is impossible, as in (i):
  (i) *John be fat? Strange!
Second, modals are not allowed in these constructions:
  (ii) *John could/may/need leave???
For an extensive discussion of these constraints, the reader is referred to Schutze 1997. With regard to the impossibility of *be*, I simply speculate that it requires some temporal features to be present in T^0 in order to be interpretable. As T^0 in tenseless clauses is "featureless" (expressed formally by the fact that it has no index), *be* is not allowed.

[45] In Avrutin 1994, I show that pronouns interpreted as bound variables in Russian undergo LF raising to adjoin to a functional head. This head can be AgrS, which would be consistent with the theory developed in this work.

Indeed, bound variables are different from, for example, deictic pronouns precisely in their referential properties.

[46] I differ here from Giorgi and Pianese 1997 who propose that in infinitival clauses Agr and T^0 form separate projections.

It should also be noted that *for-clauses* present an apparent counterexample for the theory I develop in this section, as they do allow pronouns:
(i) For her to go to school now would be hard.
This should not be the case if infinitival clauses have no agreement features. I hypothesise that *for* takes as a complement AgrSP, which contains agreement features. The pronoun therefore is allowed in *for*-clauses, as in (i), but disallowed in headlines, as in (66).

At the same time, headlines do allow Negation (at least for some speakers):
(ii) PRESIDENT NOT TO VISIT RUSSIA
The question is what the position of Neg. is, given that there is only one AGR/T-P projection. One possibility is to assume the multiple Specifier hypothesis (Chomsky 1995). In this case both *PRESIDENT* and *NOT* would each occupy the Specifier of AGR/T-P.

[47] Notice also that the pronoun can appear only in its default, non-structural case:
(i) Him/*He dance??? Never!!
This observation is consistent with the claim that the subject of the Russian RIs shows up in its default case, which in Russian is Nominative. See discussion in Section 3.

[48] Unlike the Mad Magazine clauses, however, that also allow pronouns, children's RIs allow both Nominative and Accusative subject pronouns (Schutze and Wexler 1996). But according to the proposed theory, the structural (i.e. Nominative) case should be disallowed. I will assume that those children who at this age allow both cases have not yet figured out the default case in English. Alternatively, we may assume that these children relate the structural case to the agreement features on AGR/T-P, not to the finiteness of tense.

[49] See, however, Phillips 1995 who shows that there are some subject WHO-questions in child speech. At the moment, I have no better explanation for this finding than to assume that WHO-questions in early child speech are D-linked, an assumption that does not appear to be too far-fetched. If so, the subject does not raise at LF, does not require an index, and the unindexed AGR/T-P is allowed.

[50] For an alternative view, see Roberts 1996 who argues that children do produce infinitives in embedded clauses. My impression, however, is that the data are very limited and not entirely clear to allow interpretation in any conclusive way.

[51] Notice that the same explanation will account for the absence of RIs with *be* and modals since the subject NPs in these cases are clearly non-agentive.

[52] Rizzi also provides other examples, such as (i) and (ii).
- (i) Che cosa dire in questi casi?
  what to say in these cases?
- (ii) Penso di giocare al pallone.
  I think to play football

I have nothing to say about (ii); (i) appears to be different from RIs assuming there is subject PROarb in this construction.

[53] The ease of processing is certainly a factor in the Headline Register as well: the reader should be able to capture the headline without spending much time and resources.

[54] Klepper-Schudlo (1996) presents evidence that Polish-speaking children do not produce RIs.

[55] According to Kent (1998), the dendritic density of Broca's area reaches its full development only at the age of 72 months.

REFERENCES

Abney, S. 1987. *The English Noun Phrase in its Sentential Aspect*, Doctoral dissertation, MIT, Cambridge, Mass.

Acker, M.T. and J.E. Boland. 1993. Do Pronominal and Nominal Anaphors access potential referents differently? Poster presented at the CUNY Conference on Sentence Processing, University of Massachusetts, Amherst, MA.

Akmajan, A. 1984. Sentence Type and form-function fit. *Natural Language and Linguistic Theory*, Vol. 2, #1.

Anderson, S. R. 1986. The Typology of Anaphoric Dependencies: Icelandic (and Other) Reflexives." In L. Hellan and K.K. Christensen, eds., *Topics in Scandinavian Syntax*, Reidel, Dordrecht.

Ariel, M. 1990. *Accessing Noun-Phrase Antecedents*. Routledge, London.

Avrutin, S. 1994. The Structural Position of Bound Variables. *Linguistic Inquiry*, 25:4, 709-727.

Avrutin, S. 1994. *Psycholinguistic investigations in the theory of reference*. Ph.D. Dissertation, MIT, Cambridge, MA. Distributed by MIT Working Papers in Linguistics.

Avrutin, S. 1997. EVENTS as Units of Discourse Representation. In J. Schaeffer (ed.) *MIT Workshop on Root Infinitives*. Cambridge, MA.

Avrutin, S. and M. Babyonyshev. 1997. Obviation in Subjunctive Clauses and Agr: Evidence from Russian. *Natural Language and Linguistic Theory, 52, 2*.

Avrutin, S. and J. Cunningham. 1997. Children and Reflexivity. *Proceedings of the 21st Boston University Conference on Language Development*, Cascadilla Press, Boston.

Avrutin, S., Lubarsky, S. and J. Greene (submitted) Comprehension of Contrastive Stress by Broca's Aphasics. *Brain and Language.*

Avrutin, S. and W. Philip. 1994. Quantification in Agrammatic Aphasia. Poster presented at the 68th meeting of the Linguistic Society of America, Boston, MA.

Avrutin, S. and R. Thornton. 1994. Distributivity and Binding in Child Grammar. *Linguistic Inquiry*, 25:1, 165-171.

Avrutin, S. and K. Wexler (in press) Children's Knowledge of Subjunctive Clauses: Obviation, Binding and reference. *Language Acquisition.*

Avrutin, S. and K. Wexler. 1992. Development of Principle B in Russian: coindexation at LF and coreference. *Language Acquisition* 4, 259-306.

Baauw, S., P. Coopmans and W. Philip. 1998. The Acquisition of Pronominal Coreference in Spanish and the Clitic-Pronoun Distinction, ms. Utrecht University.

Bach, E. On Time, Tense, and Aspect: An Essay in English Metaphysics. In P. Cole, ed., *Radical Pragmatics.* New York: Academic Press. 63-81.

Bailyn, J. 1992. LF Movement of Anaphors and Acquisition of Embedded Clauses in Russian. *Language Acquisition* 4, 307-336.

Bastiaanse, R. and R. Jonkers. 1998. Verb retrieval in action naming and spontaneous speech in agrammatic and anomic speech. *Aphasiology* 12, 951-969

Bastiaanse, R. 1995. Broca's Aphasia: A syntactic and/or Morphological Disorder? A case Study. *Brain and Language*, 48, 1-32.

Bastiaanse, R. and R. van Zonneveld. 1998. On the Relation between Verb Inflection and Verb Position in Dutch Agrammatic Aphasics. *Brain and Language* 64, 165-181.

Behrens, H. 1994. *Temporal Reference in German Child Language.* Ph.D. Dissertation, University of Amsterdam

Bennett, J. 1988. *Events and their names*. Hackett Press, Indianapolis.

Berwick, R. 1985. *The Acquisition of Syntactic Knowledge*, MIT Press, Cambridge.

Bloom, P., A. Barss, J. Nicol and L. Conway. 1994. Children's Knowledge of Binding and Coreference: Evidence from Spontaneous Speech. *Language* 70, pp. 53-72.

Boser, K., B. Lust, L. Santelman and J. Whitman. 1992. The syntax of CP and V-2 in early child German: The strong continuity hypothesis. In K. Broderick (ed.), *Proceedings of NELS 23*, 51-65, Amherst, Mass.: GSLA

Bromberger, H. and K. Wexler. 1995. Null subjects in declaratives and wh-questions. In MIT Working Papers in Linguistics, Vol. 2.

Cairns, H.S., McDaniel, D., Hsu, D., and R. Michelle. 1994. A longitudinal study of principles of control and pronominal reference in child English. *Language, 70*, 260-288.

Caramazza, A. and E. B. Zurif. 1978. *Language Acquisition and Language Breakdown*. The Johns Hopkins University Press, Baltimore.

Cardinaletti A. and M. Starke. 1993. On Dependent Pronouns and Pronoun Movement. Paper presented at the GLOW conference, Lund.

Chien, Y.-C. and K. Wexler. 1991. Children's knowledge of locality conditions in Binding as evidence for the modularity of syntax and pragmatics. *Language Acquisition* 1:225-295.

Chomsky, N. 1981. *Lectures on Government and Binding*. Foris, Dordrecht.

Chomsky, N. 1986a. *Knowledge of Language: Its Nature, Origin, and Use.* New York: Praeger.

Chomsky, N. 1995. *The Minimalist Program*. MIT Press. Cambridge, MA.

Clark, E. 1977. From Gesture to Word: On the Natural History of Deixis in Language Acquisition. In *Human Growth and Development: Wolfson College Lectures 1976*. J.S. Bruner and A.Garton (eds.). Oxford Unviersity Press.

Clark, H. 1977. Bridging. In Johnson-Laird, P. and P. Wason (eds.), *Thinking*. Cambridge University Press, Cambridge, pp. 411-420.

Clark, H. and S. Haviland. 1977. Comprehension and the Given-New Contract," in R. Freedle (ed.), *Discoure Production and Comprehension*. Norwood, N.J.: Ablex, 1-40.

Clark, H. and C. Marshall. 1981. Definite Reference and Mutual Knowledge, in A.K. Joshi et al (eds), pp. 10-63.

Clements, N. 1975. The Logophoric Pronoun in Ewe: Its Role in Discourse. *Journal of West African Languages* 10, 141-177.

Crain, S. 1992. "Language Acquisition in the Absence of Experience", *Behavioral and Brain Sciences* 14, 597-650.

Crain, S. and C. McKee (1985). "Acquisition of Structural Restrictions on Anaphora", *Proceedings of NELS 16*, 94-110.

Crain, S.& R. Thornton (1998*) Investigations in Universal Grammar: A Guide to Experiments on the Acquisition of Syntax and Semantics*, MIT Press, Cambridge, Mass.

Crain, S. and K. Wexler. 1994. Methodology in the Study of Language Acquisition: A MInimalist/Modular Approach. To appear in: W.C. Ritchie and T.K. Bhatia (eds.), *Handbook of Language Acquisition*, Academic Press.

Crisma, P. 1992. On the acquisition of Wh-questions in French. *Geneva Generative Papers* 1992, 115-122.

Davidson, D. 1980. *Essays on Actions and Events*. Clarendon Press, Oxford.

Dell, F. 1981. On the learnability of optional phonological rules. *Linguistic Inquiry* 12, 31-37.

De Villiers, G. and P. De Villiers. 1978. *Language Acquisition*. Harvard University Press.

REFERENCES

Enç, M. 1991. Anchoring Conditions for Tense. *Linguistic Inquiry,* 18, 633-657.

Fiengo, R. and R. May. 1993. *Indices and Identity.* MIT Press, Cambridge, MA.

Foster-Cohen, S.H. 1994. Exploring the Boundary Between Syntax and Pragmatics: Relevance and the Binding of Pronouns. Journal of Child Language, 21, pp. 237-255.

Frege, G. 1892. On Sense and Reference. In F. Zabeeh et al (eds.) (1974), pp. 117- 140.

Giorgi, A. and F. Pianesi. 1997. *From Semantics to Morphosyntax.* Cambridge.

Gleason, J.B. et al. 1975. The retrieval of syntax in Broca's aphasia. *Brain and Language,* 2, 451-471.

Goodglass, H. and N. Geschwind. 1976. Language disorders (aphasia). In *Handbook of Perception,* Vol. 7

Grimshaw, J. and S. T. Rosen 1990. Knowledge and obedience: The developmental status of the Binding Theory. *Linguistic Inquiry* 21:187-222.

Grober, E.H., W. Beardsley and A. Caramazza. 1978. Parallel Function Strategy in Pronoun Assignment. *Cognition* 6, p.. 117-135.

Grodzinsky, Y. 1990. Theoretical Perspectives on Language Deficit. MIT Press, Cambridge.

Grodzinsky, Y. and T. Reinhart. 1993. The innateness of Binding and the development of coreference", *Linguistic Inquiry* 24:69-103.

Grodzinsky, Y., K. Wexler, Chien, Y.-C., S. Marakovitz and J. Solomon. 1993. The breakdown of binding relations. *Brain and Language,* 45, 371-395.

Gueron, J. and T. Hoekstra. 1995. The temporal interpretation of predication. In A. Cardinaletti and T. Guasti (eds.) *Syntax and Semantics,* 28. Academic Press.

Haegeman, L. 1994. Root Infinitives, Tense, and truncated Structures of Dutch. *Language Acquisition*, 4, 205-255

Hawkins, J. 1978. *Definiteness and Indefiniteness.* London: Croom Helm.

Heim, I. 1982. The Semantics of Definite and Indefinite Noun Phrases. PhD Dissertation, University of Massachusetts, Amherst, MA.

Heim, I. 1993. Anaphora and Semantic Interpretation: A Reinterpretation of Reinhart's Approach. SfS-Report-07-93. University of Tubingen.

Heim, I., H. Lasnik and R. May. 1991. Reciprocity and plurality. *Linguistic Inquiry* 22:63- 102.

Hellan, L. 1988. *Anaphora in Norwegian and the Theory of Grammar.* Foris, Dordrecht.

Hestvik, A. 1990. *LF-Movement of Pronouns and the Computation of Binding Domains.* Doctoral dissertation, Brandeis University, Waltham, Mass.

Hestvik, A. 1991. "Subjectless Binding Domains", *Natural Language and Linguistic Theory* 9, 455-496.

Hestvik, A. 1992. LF-Movement of Pronouns and Anti-Subject Orientation. *Linguistic Inquiry* 23, 557-594.

Higginbotham, J. 1985. "On Semantics", *Linguistic Inquiry* 16, 574-594.

Hyams, N. 1986. *Language Acquisition and the Theory of Parameters*, Reidel Dordrecht.

Hyams, N. 1996. The Underspecification of Functional Categories in Early Grammar. In H. Clahsen (ed.) *Generative Perspective on Language Acquisition.* John Benjamins: Amsterdam.

Ingram, D. and W. Thompson. 1996. Early Syntactic Acquisition in German: Evidence for the Modal Hypothesis. *Language*, 72, 97-120.

Jakobson, R. 1941/1968. Child Language, Aphasia, and Phonological Universals. Mouton, the Hague.

Jakubowicz, C. 1984. On Markedness and Binding Principles. Proceedings of NELS 14, 154-182.

Jantke, K.P. (ed.). 1986. International Workshop AII '86. Analogical and Inductive Inference: Proceedings. Berlin.

Jarema, G. and D. Kadzielawa. 1990. Agrammatism in Polish: A case Study. In L. Menn and L. Obler (eds.): *Agrammatic aphasia: A cross-language narrative sourcebook.* John Benjamin's Publishing Company, Philadelphia.

Kamp, H. and U. Reyle. 1993. *From Discourse to Logic.* Kluwer, Dordrecht.

Karmiloff-Smith, A. 1981. The Grammatical Marking of Thematic Structure in the Development of Language Production. In W. Deutch (ed.), *The Child's Construction of Language.* London: Academic Press.

Kent, R.D. 1998. Chronology of Speech Subsystem Development. Talk given at Haskins Laboratories, New Haven, CT.

Klein, W. 1994. *Time in Language.* London: Kluwer.

Klepper-Schudlo, A. 1996. Early verbal inflection in Polish and the optional infinitive phenomenon. Talk presented at the Workshop on the Acquisition of Morphology in L2. Seventh International Morphology Meeting, Austria.

Kolk, H. and C. Heeschen. 1990. Adaptation and Impairment Symptoms in Broca's Aphasia. Aphasiology, 4, 221-232.

Kolk, H. and C. Heeschen. 1992. Agrammatism, Paragrammatism and the Management of Language. *Language and Cognitive Processes*, 7, 89-129.

Koster, C. 1993. *Errors in Anaphora Acquisition.* Utrecht University, The Netherlands.

Kramer, I. 1993. The licensing of subjects in early child language. In C. Phillips (ed.) *Papers on Case and Agreement II,* MITWPL 19, 197-212.

Kratzer, A. 1989. Stage and Individual level Predicates. *Papers on Quantification.* UMASS, Amherst.

Kuno, S. 1972. Pronominalization, Reflexivization, and Direct Discourse. *Linguistic Inquiry,* 3, 161-196.

Kuroda, Y. 1988. "Whether We Agree or Not," *Lingvisticae Investigationes* 12, 1-47.

Lasnik, H. 1989. *Essays on Anaphora,* Kluwer, Dordrecht.

Lasnik, H. and S. Crain. 1985. On the acquisition of pronominal reference. *Lingua* 65:135-154.

Lebeaux, D. 1988. *Language Acquisition and the Form of the Grammar.* Ph.D. dissertation, University of Massachusetts, Amherst.

Lesser, R. and M. Milroy. 1993. *Linguistics and Aphasia.* Longman, London.

Link, G. 1983. The logical analysis of plurals and mass terms: A lattice- theoretical approach. In *Meaning, use and interpretation of language.,* eds. Rainer Bauerle et al., 302-323. Berlin: de Gruyter.

Link, G. 1987. Generalized quantifiers and plurals. In *Generalized quantifiers: linguistic and logical approaches,* ed. Peter Gärdenfors, 151-180. Dordrecht: D. Reidel.

Lust, B., Eisele, J. and R. Mazuka. 1992. "The Binding Theory Module: Evidence from First language Acquisition for Principle C", *Language* 2, 333-358.

Mailing, J. 1984. Non-clause-bounded Reflexives in Modern Icelandic. *Linguistic and Philosophy* 7, 211-241.

Mailing, J. 1986. Clause-bounded Reflexives in Modern Icelandic. In L. Hellan and K.K. Christensen, eds., *Topics in Scandinavian Syntax,* Reidel, Dordrecht.

REFERENCES

McWhinney, B. and C. Snow. 1985. The Child Language Data Exchange System. Journal of Child Language 12, pp. 271-296.

Marantz, A. 1984. *On the Nature of Grammatical Relations*, Cambridge, MA: MIT Press.

Maratsos, M. 1973. The Effect of Stress on the Understanding of Pronominal Coreference in Children. Journal of Psycholinguistic Research 2, pp. 1-8.

Maratsos, M. 1976. *The Use of Definite and Indefinite Reference in Young Children*. Cambridge University Press, Cambridge.

Maxfield, T. and D. McDaniel. 1992. "Principle B and Contrastive Stress," *Language Acquisition* 4.

McDaniel, D., H. S. Cairns and J. R. Hsu. 1990. Binding principles in the grammars of young children. *Language Acquisition* 1:121-139.

McKee, C. 1992. "A Comparison of Pronouns and Anaphors in Italian and English Acquisition", *Language Acquisition* 1, 21-55.

Menn, L. and L.K.Obler (eds.) 1990. *Agrammatic aphasia: A cross-language narrative sourcebook*. John Benjamin's Publishing Company, Philadelphia.

Miyamoto, Y. and S. Crain. 1991. Children's interpretation of plural pronouns: collective vs. distributive interpretation. Paper presented at the 16th Annual Boston University Conference on Language Development, October, 1991.

Miceli, G. and A. Mazuzuchi. 1990. Agrammatism in Italian. In L. Menn and L. Obler (eds.): *Agrammatic aphasia: A cross-language narrative sourcebook*. John Benjamin's Publishing Company, Philadelphia.

Montalbetti, M.M. and K. Wexler. 1988. "Binding is Linking," *Proceedings of the West Coast Conference on Formal Linguistics* 4, 228-245.

Mussan, R. 1995. *On the Temporal Interpretation of Noun Phrases*. Ph.D. Dissertation, MIT, Cambridge, MA.

Nespoulos, J.-L, M. Dordain, C. Perron, G. Jarema, and M. Chazal. 1990. Agrammatism in French: Two case studies. In L. Menn and L. Obler (eds.): *Agrammatic aphasia: A cross-language narrative sourcebook*. John Benjamin's Publishing Company, Philadelphia.

Otsu, Y. 1981. *Universal Grammar and Syntactic Development in Children: Towards a theory of syntactic development*, Doctoral dissertation, MIT, Cambridge, MA.

Padilla, J. 1990. *On the Definition of Binding Domains in Spanish*. Kluwer, Dordrecht.

Paris, S.G. and Lindauer, B.K. 1976. The Role of Inference in Children's Comprehension and Memory for Sentences. *Cognitive Psychology*, 8, 217- 227.

Parsons, T. 1990. Events in the Semantics of English: A study in subatomic semantics. MIT Press.

Partee, B. 1973. Some structural analogies between tenses and pronouns in English. *The Journal of Philosophy*, vo.l LXX, No. 18.

Pesetsky, D. 1987. "Wh-in-situ: Movement and Unselective Binding," in Reuland, E. and A. ter Meulen, eds., *The Representation of (In)definiteness*, MIT Press, Cambridge,

Phillips, C. 1995. Syntax at the age of two: Cross-Linguistic Differences. In MIT Working Papers in Linguistics, Vol. 2. (325-382)

Pianesi, F. and A. Varzi. 1996. Refining Temporal Reference in Event Structures. *Notre Dame Journal of Formal Logic*. 37(1).

Pica, P. 1987. On the Nature of the Reflexivization Cycle. In *Proceedings of NELS*, 17.

Pierce, A. 1992. *Language Acquisition and Syntactic Theory: Comparative Analysis of French and English Child Grammars*, Kluwer, Dordrecht.

Pinon, C. 1996. *An Ontology of Events*. Ph.D. dissertation, Stanford University.

REFERENCES

Poeppel, D. and K. Wexler. 1993. The Full Competence Hypothesis of Clause Structure, Language, 69.

Radford, A. *Syntactic Theory and the Acquisition of English Syntax: The Nature of Early Child Grammars of English.* Oxford: Basil Blackwell.

Reichenbach, H. 1947. *Elements of Symbolic Logic.* London: Macmillan.

Reinhart, T. 1983. *Anaphora and Semantic Interpretation.* London: Croom Helm.

Reinhart, T. 1986. Center and Periphery in the Grammar of Anaphora. In *Studies in the Acquisition of Anaphora,* Barbara Lust *ed.,* , vol. I. Dordrecht: Reidel.

Reinhart, T. and E. Reuland. 1993. Reflexivity. *Linguistic Inquiry,* 24, 657-720.

Ribot, T.A. 1883. *Les maladies de la memoire.* Libraire Germain Bailliere, Paris.

Rizzi, L. 1994. Some Notes on Linguistic Theory and Language Development: The Case of Root Infinitives. *Language Acquisition* 3, 371 - 393.

Roberts, C. 1987. *Modal subordination, anaphora and distributivity.* Doctoral dissertation, University of Massachusetts, Amherst.

Roberts, T. 1996. Evidence for the Optional Tense Hypothesis: Tense in subordinate Clauses in the Acquisition of English. Paper presented at WECOL, UC Santa Cruz.

Roeper, T. and B. Rohrbacher. 1994. Null subjects in early child language and the theory of economy of projection. ms. University of Massachusetts and University of Pennsylvania .

Roo, E. de. 1998. A Dummy Tense Element in Agrammatic Speech? In S. Barbiers, J. Rooryck and J. van de Weijer (eds.) *Small Words in the Big Picture.* Holland Institute of Generative Linguistics.

Sag, I. 1977. *Deletion and Logical Form*, PhD Dissertation., MIT, Cambridge.

Schaeffer, J. (ed.) 1997. *Proceedings of the MIT Workshop on Root Infinitives.* Cambridge, MA.

Schutze, C. and K. Wexler. 1996. Subject Case Licensing and Root Infinitives. In A. Stringfellow et al (eds.). *Proceedings of the 20th Annual Boston University Conference on Language Development.* Somerville, MA: Cascadilla Press, Somerville, 670-681.

Schutze, C. 1997. *INFL Character in Child and Adult Language: Agreement, Case and Licensing.* Ph.D. Dissertation, MIT.

Sells, P. 1987. Aspects of Logophoricity. *Linguistic Inquiry,* 18, 445-481.

Sigurjonsdottir, S. and Hyams, N. 1992. Reflexivization and Logophoricity: Evidence from the Acquisition of Icelandic. *Language Acquisition,* vol. 2 #4, pp. 359-413.

Solan, L. 1983. *Pronominal Reference: Child Language and the Theory of Grammar.* Reidel, Dordreht.

Sperber, D. and D. Wilson. 1986. *Relevance.* Cambridge, MA: Harvard University Press.

Stowell, T. 1996. Empty Heads in Abbreviated English. (ms.) UCLA.

Swinney, D. 1979. Lexical Access during Sentence Comprehension: (Re)consideration of Context Effects. *Journal of Verbal Learning and Verbal Behavior,* 18, pp. 645-659.

Swinney, D., J. Nicol and E. Zurif. 1989. The Effects of Focal Brain Damage on Sentence Processing: An Examination of the Neurological Organization of a Mental Module. *Journal of Cognitive Neuroscience,* 1, pp. 25-37.

Swinney, D. and P. Prather. 1989. On the Comprehension of Lexical Ambiguity by Young Children: Investigations into the Development of Mental Modularity. In *Resolving Semantic Ambiguity,* ed. D. Gorfein. New York: Springer Verlag.

Tavokolian, S. 1978. Children's Comprehension of Pronominal Subjects and Missing Subjects in Complicated Sentences. In H. Goodluck and L. Solan (eds.), *Papers in the Structure and*

Development of Child Language. University of Massachusetts Occasional Papers in Linguistics, vol. 4.

Thornton, R. 1990. *Adventures in Long-distance Movement: The Acquisition of Complex Wh-Questions.* Doctoral dissertation, The University of Connecticut, Storrs.

Thornton, R. and K. Wexler. (in press). *VP Ellipsis, the Binding Theory and Interpretation in Child Grammar.*

Vainikka, A. 1994. Case in the development of English. *Language Acquisition* 3, 257-325.

Valian, V. 1991.Syntactic Subjects in the Early Speech of American and Italian Children. *Cognition.*, 40, 21-81.

Vendler, Z. 1967. Verbs and Times. *Philosophical Review* 66, 143-160.

Wales, R. 1986. Deixis. In P. Fletcher and M. Garman (eds.) *Language Acquisition.* Cambridge University Press, Cambridge.

Warden, D.A. 1976. The Influence of Context on Children's Use of Identifying Expressions and References. *British Journal of Psychology*, 67, pp. 101-112.

Weissenborn, J. and W. Klein. 1982. *Here and There: Crosslinguistic Studies on Deixis and Demonstration.* Benjamins, Amsterdam.

Weverink, M. 1989. *The subject in relation to inflection in child language.* MA Thesis. University of Utrecht.

Wexler, K. and R. Manzini. 1987. "Parameters and Learnability in Binding Theory", in T. Roeper and E. Williams, eds., *Parameter Setting*, Reidel, Dordrecht.

Wexler, K. and Y.-C. Chien. 1985. "The Development of Lexical Anaphors and Pronouns", *Papers and Reports on Child Language Development 24*, Stanford University, 138-149.

Wexler, K. and Y.-C. Chien. 1988. "The Acquisition of Locality Principles in Binding Theory", paper presented at the 11th Generative Linguists of the Old World Colloquium (GLOW), Budapest, Hungary.

Wexler, K. 1995. Optional Infinitives, Head Movement and the Economy of Derivation in Child Grammar. In D. Lightfoot and N. Hosrnstein (eds.) *Verb Movement..* Cambridge University Press.

Wijnen, F. 1997. The Temporal Interpretation of Root Infinitivals in Dutch. *Proceedings of the MIT Workshop on Root Infinitives.*

Williams, E. 1977. Discourse and Logical Form. *Linguistic Inquiry* 8, 101-139.

Winston, P.H. 1991. *Artificial Intelligence.* Addison-Wesley Publishing Company.

Wykes, T. 1981. Inference and Children's Comprehension of Pronouns. Journal of Experimental Child Psychology, 32, pp. 264-278.

Zribi-Hertz, A. 1989. A-type binding and narrative point of view. *Language* 65.4, 695-727.

NAME INDEX

Abney 84
Acker 69
Akmajan 158
Anderson 108
Ariel 47, 151, 184fn
Avrutin 16, 20, 36, 79, 83, 94, 152, 187fn
Baauw 186fn
Bach 140
Bailyn 15
Bastiaanse 173
Beardsley 78
Behrens 146
Bennett 140
Berwick 14, 180
Bloom 63
Boland 69
Boser 133
Bromberger 167
Cairns 66, 73
Caramazza 78, 179
Cardinaletti 15, 66

Chien 9, 17, 36
Chomsky 9, 12, 25, 85, 115, 133, 141
Clark, E 184fn
Clark, H 42
Clements 103, 107
Coopmans 186fn
Crain 66, 99, 186fn
Crisma 167
Cunningham 188fn
Davidson 140
Dell 180
De Roo 173
De Villiers, G 74
De Villiers, P 74
Dowty 141
Eisele 66
Enç 143, 189fn
Fiengo 190fn
Foster-Cohen 15
Frege 27
Geschwind 172

NAME INDEX

Giorgi 146, 156, 160, 163, 189fn

Gleason 172

Goodglass 172

Grimshaw 17. 101

Grober 78

Grodzinsky 18, 20, 137, 180

Gueron 135, 141, 150

Haegeman 138

Hawkins 39, 47, 184fn

Heeschen 173

Heim 9, 23, 27, 30, 33, 46, 94, 184fn, 190fn

Hellan 108

Hestvik 15, 83

Higginbotham 27, 65, 140

Hoekstra 135, 141, 150

Hsu 66

Hyams 15, 111, 124, 135, 142, 167, 188fn

Ingram 133, 168

Jakobson 179

Jakubowicz 16

Jantke 184fn

Jarema 175

Jonkers 173

Kadzielawa 175

Karmiloff-Smith 75

Kamp 140

Kent 192fn

Klein 170, 187fn

Klepper-Schudlo 192fn

Kolk 173

Koster 16

Kramer 136

Kratzer 147, 157

Kuno 109

Lasnik 25, 94, 99

Lebeaux 133

Lesser 172

Lindauer 81

Link 95

Lust 66

MacWhinney 74

Mailing 108

Manzini 14, 180

Marantz 111

Maratsos 74, 78

Marshall 42

Maxfield 79

May 94, 190fn

Mazuzuchi 175

Mazuka 66

NAME INDEX

McDaniel 66, 79
McKee 66, 79
Menn 172
Miceli 175
Milroy 172
Miyamoto 99. 188fn
Montalbetti 184fn
Mussan 147
Nespoulos 172
Nicol 20, 82
Obler 172
Padilla 120, 124
Paris 81
Parsons 140, 144
Partee 136
Pesetsky 150
Philip 186fn
Phillips 135, 167, 169
Pianesi 146, 156, 160, 163, 189fn
Pica 15
Pierce 132, 173
Pinon 140
Poeppel 135, 173
Prather 20, 32
Radford 132, 133
Reichenbach 154
Reinhart 18, 19, 27, 29, 104, 110, 137
Reuland 104, 110
Reyle 140
Ribot 179
Rizzi 133, 169
Roberts, C. 95
Roberts, T. 192fn
Roeper 167
Rohrbacher 167
Rosen, 17, 101
Sag 18
Sells 103, 107, 109
Schaeffer 135
Schutze 152, 158, 190fn
Sigurjonsdottir 15, 111
Snow 74
Solan 186fn
Sperber 15
Starke 15, 66
Stowell 152, 153
Swinney 20, 82
Tavokolian 186fn
Thompson 133, 168
Thornton 65, 94, 186fn, 187fn

Vainika 133

Valian 168

Varzi 146

Vendler 147, 156

Wales 187fn

Warden 74

Weissenborn 187fn

Weverink 132

Wexler 9, 14, 16, 20, 36, 133, 167, 173, 180, 186fn

Wijnen 168

Williams 18

Wilson 15

Winston 184fn

Wykes 81

Zonneveld 174

Zribi-Hertz 108

Zurif 20, 82, 179

SUBJECT INDEX

accommodation 23, 42, 44, 69

accomplishment predicates 156

accessibility 151

achievement predicates 160

agentivity 150

associative use 49

ambiguous words 82

auxiliary 167, 173

binding theory 9, 12

bound variables 19, 30, 95,

bridging 42, 44, 46, 52, 57, 71, 92

Broca's aphasics, 10, 19, 64, 79, 81, 172, 174

case 139, 152, 191fn

center of discourse 112, 115, 123, 129

cohesion 73

common ground 123

conversation-internal knowledge 8, 50, 111

deixis 9, 47, 48, 59, 62, 187fn

discourse time presupposition 148

distributive operator 95

Dutch 116, 133, 168, 173, 174

egocentricity 77

encyclopedic knowledge 52

events 140

    boundaries of 146, 148, 156, 159, 160

    resultant (consequent) 144, 159

    in-progress 144

    culminated 144

    definite 160, 162

    topologically closed 146, 161

event time 154

features 11, 133, 141, 156, 163

file cards,

    individual 31, 34, 108, 141, 189fn

    events 140, 144, 175

    and reference 32

    situation 49, 52

SUBJECT INDEX

projection of 145, 146

resultant 145

File Change Semantics 9, 23, 30, 93, 123

French 73, 132

German 132, 173

guises 23, 28, 32, 34, 36

    and indices 28

    identity of 28, 36

headlines 152, 155, 163

Icelandic 13, 15, 108

Immediate situation use 39, 47

incorporation 23, 42, 44, 62, 67, 69, 110

indexation 22, 26, 142, 166, 167, 184fn, 190fn

    interpretation of 32

individual level predicates 147, 148, 157, 158

inferences 13, 50, 53, 58, 159

instantiation 33, 34, 44, 144, 170

    rules for 45

Italian 65, 156, 169, 171, 175, 192fn

Japanese 109

knowledge implementation 10, 183

larger situation use 39, 47

learnability 14

life time effect 147

locative prepositions 111

logophors 104, 106, 115, 120

Mad Magazine register 158, 160, 164

modality 153, 168, 173

Optional Infinitive stage 132

picture NP 114

plural pronouns 93

pointing 57, 68

Polish 175, 192fn

presupposition 157, 165

principle P 17, 21, 36

priming 20, 81

processing resources 20, 22, 58, 77, 78, 111, 124, 170

quantifiers ,

    generalised 18

    as antecedents 21, 62

    in root infinitives 139, 149, 158

reference 22, 26, 27, 29, 70

reference time 155

referential potential 141, 189fn

reflexivity, theory 105

regression hypothesis 179

relevance, theory of 15

root infinitives 135, 138, 143, 145, 168

rule I 18, 19, 137

rule T 137

Russian 13, 15, 83, 85, 138, 145, 149, 164

      possessive pronouns in 13, 83, 91

sense 27, 28

Spanish 124

speaker-internal rules 50, 111

speaker-internal knowledge 8, 13

speech time 141, 155

stress 78, 79

strong pronouns 64, 65

subjunctive 13, 20, 150

subset principle 14, 180

tense 133, 135, 153

tense chain 141, 150, 154, 162, 167

truncation 135

underspecification 135

visible/invisible situations 77

weak pronouns 64

Wernicke's aphasics 20

STUDIES IN THEORETICAL PSYCHOLINGUISTICS

1. L. Solan: *Pronominal Reference.* Child Language and the Theory of Grammar. 1983 ISBN 90-277-1495-9
2. B. Lust (ed.): *Studies in the Acquisition of Anaphora.* Volume I: Defining the Constraints. 1986 ISBN 90-277-2121-1; Pb 90-277-2122-X
3. N. M. Hyams: *Language Acquisition and the Theory of Parameters.* 1986 ISBN 90-277-2218-8; Pb 90-277-2219-6
4. T. Roeper and E. Williams (eds.): *Parameter Setting.* 1987 ISBN 90-277-2315-X; Pb 90-277-2316-8
5. S. Flynn: *A Parameter-Setting Model of L2 Acquisition.* Experimental Studies in Anaphora. 1987 ISBN 90-277-2374-5; Pb 90-277-2375-3
6. B. Lust (ed.): *Studies in the Acquisition of Anaphora.* Volume II: Applying the Constraints. 1987 ISBN 1-55608-022-0; Pb 1-55608-023-9
7. G. N. Carlson and M. K. Tanenhaus (eds.): *Linguistic Structure in Language Processing.* 1989 ISBN 1-55608-074-3; Pb 1-55608-075-1
8. S. Flynn and W. O'Neil (eds.): *Linguistic Theory in Second Language Acquisition.* 1988 ISBN 1-55608-084-0; Pb 1-55608-085-9
9. R. J. Matthews and W. Demopoulos (eds.): *Learnability and Linguistic Theory.* 1989 ISBN 0-7923-0247-8; Pb 0-7923-0558-2
10. L. Frazier and J. de Villiers (eds.): *Language Processing and Language Acquisition.* 1990 ISBN 0-7923-0659-7; Pb 0-7923-0660-0
11. J.A. Padilla: *On the Definition of Binding Domains in Spanish.* Evidence from Child Language. 1990 ISBN 0-7923-0744-5
12. M. de Vincenzi: *Syntactic Parsing Strategies in Italian.* The Minimal Chain Principle. 1991 ISBN 0-7923-1274-0; Pb 0-7923-1275-9
13. D.C. Lillo-Martin: *Universal Grammar and American Sign Language.* Setting the Null Argument Parameters. 1991 ISBN 0-7923-1419-0
14. A.E. Pierce: *Language Acquisition and Syntactic Theory.* A Comparative Analysis of French and English Child Grammars. 1992 ISBN 0-7923-1553-7
15. H. Goodluck and M. Rochemont (eds.): *Island Constraints.* Theory, Acquisition and Processing. 1992 ISBN 0-7923-1689-4
16. J.M. Meisel (ed.): *The Acquisition of Verb Placement.* Functional Categories and V2 Phenomena in Language Acquisition. 1992 ISBN 0-7923-1906-0
17. E.C. Klein: *Toward Second Language Acquisition.* A Study of Null-Prep. 1993 ISBN 0-7923-2463-3

STUDIES IN THEORETICAL PSYCHOLINGUISTICS

18. J.L. Packard: *A Linguistic Investigation of Aphasic Chinese Speech.* 1993
 ISBN 0-7923-2466-8
19. J. Archibald: *Language Learnability and L2 Phonology:* The Acquisition of Metrical Parameters. 1993 ISBN 0-7923-2486-2
20. M.W. Crocker: *Computational Psycholinguistics.* An Interdisciplinary Approach to the Study of Language. 1996 ISBN 0-7923-3802-2; Pb 0-7923-3806-5
21. J.D. Fodor and F. Ferreira (eds.): *Reanalysis in Sentence Processing.* 1998
 ISBN 0-7923-5099-5
22. L. Frazier: *On Sentence Interpretation.* 1999 ISBN 0-7923-5508-3

KLUWER ACADEMIC PUBLISHERS – DORDRECHT / BOSTON / LONDON